NEW REALMS

Inspire Student Expression
with *Digital Age Formats*

International Society for Technology in Education
PORTLAND, OREGON • ARLINGTON, VIRGINIA

MICHELE HAIKEN

For my students past, present, and future.

NEW REALMS FOR WRITING

Inspire Student Expression with Digital Age Formats

Michele Haiken

Senior Acquisitions Editor: Valerie Witte
Development and Copy Editor: Linda Laflamme
Proofreader: Lisa Hein
Indexer: Wendy Allex
Book Design and Production: Danielle Foster
Cover Design: Edwin Ouellette

Library of Congress Cataloging-in-Publication Data available

First Edition
ISBN: 978-1-56484-790-4
Ebook version available

Printed in the United States of America

ISTE® is a registered trademark of the International Society for Technology in Education.

About ISTE

The International Society for Technology in Education (ISTE) is a nonprofit organization that works with the global education community to accelerate the use of technology to solve tough problems and inspire innovation. Our worldwide network believes in the potential technology holds to transform teaching and learning.

ISTE sets a bold vision for education transformation through the ISTE Standards, a framework for students, educators, administrators, coaches and computer science educators to rethink education and create innovative learning environments. ISTE hosts the annual ISTE Conference & Expo, one of the world's most influential ed tech events. The organization's professional learning offerings include online courses, professional networks, year-round academies, peer-reviewed journals and other publications. ISTE is also the leading publisher of books focused on technology in education. For more information or to become an ISTE member, visit iste.org. Subscribe to ISTE's YouTube channel and connect with ISTE on Twitter, Facebook and LinkedIn.

Related ISTE Titles

Personalized Reading: Digital Strategies and Tools to Support All Learners

Michele Haiken with L. Robert Furman

To see all books available from ISTE, please visit iste.org/books.

About the Author

MICHELE HAIKEN, ED.D. is the author behind *The Teaching Factor* (theteachingfactor.com), a weekly blog on all things literacy and digital technology that help strengthen student learning. A lifelong bookworm, Michele has been teaching middle-school English for twenty years and adjuncting as professor of literacy for twelve years. She is co-author of *Personalized Reading: Digital Strategies and Tools to Support All Learners* and the editor of the book *Gamify Literacy*. Her writing has appeared in blogs for *ISTE, School Library Journal, Q & A with Larry Ferlazzo, Free Tech 4 Teachers*, and *The Nerdy Book Club*. She presents workshops and webinars on the subjects of literacy, technology, and gamification at conferences around the United States. A member of ISTE's Literacy PLN, she moderates #ISTELitChat, a monthly Twitter chat discussing digital literacy. She lives in Stamford, Connecticut, with her family. You can connect with her on Twitter @teachingfactor.

Acknowledgments

It starts with an idea, but then it takes a conversation, a written proposal, more discussions, reading and writing, reviewing, editing, and revisions to bring a book to publication. And that is just on the writer's end. Thank you to everyone at ISTE publishing who continues to support my ideas and helped bring this book to fruition. I greatly acknowledge my editor, Valerie Witte, who always listens to my ideas and knows how to ask just the right questions that push my writing to new realms. Linda Laflamme, you are an amazing copy editor who makes me a better writer with your critical eye and keen sense of the power of words on a page.

I am grateful to my mentors and friends, whom I depend on for feedback and encouragement: Mark Gura, Peter Gouveia, Christine Balsama, and Yvette Rivera. Additionally, my PLN has been invaluable to help me learn and grow professionally.

Thank you to my colleagues at Rye Middle School. Together we share a commitment to making learning meaningful. Our conversations and reflections on teaching and learning always inspire me and help me look at students, curriculum, and teaching with new perspectives and possibilities. I am grateful to my grade-level teammates and colleagues Jim, Lisa, James, Michelle, Suzanne, and Francesca for sharing their teaching practices and collaborating with me. In particular, I want to thank my principal, Dr. Ann Edwards, for her continued support.

To my students at Rye Middle School and Manhattanville College: Thank you for listening, writing, raising questions, and sharing your ideas. This book wouldn't hold any weight without your writing and discussions about writing in our classroom. As I write alongside you, know that your words matter and your voice needs to be heard.

Acknowledgments

Most importantly, thank you to my family who inspires, cheers, and allows me to write. Jennifer, Nick, Yael, and Matthew, you always offer insight and are encouraging me. Mom and Dad, you provide me with continuous support. EJ, you keep me grounded with your patience and endless support while I am feverishly writing. I am grateful for all that you do for me and our family. Max and Sadie, I am blessed with the both of you. You are great storytellers and wise beyond your years. Know the ocean is filled with stories. Listen and learn from these stories, and then make sure to write your own voyage. I am excited for more adventures ahead.

Contents

 # Foreword

Last summer, during a few brief moments that I had to stand in the ISTE bookstore before rushing off to my next event, a title caught my eye: Michele Haiken's recently released *Personalized Reading: Digital Strategies and Tools to Support All Learners* (with L. Robert Furman). Next to that, I saw her *Gamify Literacy: Boost Comprehension, Collaboration and Learning*. And, then remembering that I had first encountered Michele's work on podcasting in Mark Gura's 2014 *Teaching Literacy in the Digital Age*, I realized that I was a fan of her work… long before I knew I was a fan of her work.

Needless to say, I was late to my next session.

As a middle-school educator and consultant, Michele understands exactly what it means to create lessons that engage her students both academically and emotionally. She notes her own struggles with writing as a student and asks, poignantly, "In this day and age, why relegate our students to writing essays?" She asks this question not as a rhetorical exercise, however, as she then firmly situates her response in a conversation about the standards we are expected to help students meet. As just one element of her overall argument, I appreciate how the ISTE and Common Core standards are woven throughout the book to show specific connections that educators can make in their plans.

Yet standards are not the only, or even the main, focus in this book. Again, as a teacher educator and someone connected through her own PLNs, ISTE, and more, I see how she has drawn strength from the examples of other teachers. Throughout the book, Michele draws in the voices—and examples—of other educators, tying them to her overall argument that "[o]ur students are creators in their own right as video producers, songwriters, bloggers, gamers, and storytellers." The examples she shares clearly demonstrate these points.

Moreover, as a literacy and language arts teacher, Michele is immersed in a process-oriented pedagogy, renewing our time tested–practices of mini-lessons and mentor texts with a multimodal spin. As much as I live and work in the tech/literacy world, Michele still shared some "new to me" tools such as TimeLooper and ZapWorks, Soundtrap and Ginger. Yet she does so in the service of literacy learning, pairing these tools with incredible mentor texts such as *The New York Times'* Anatomy of a Scene video series and numerous podcasts. At heart, she is a teacher of language, and this comes through in every lesson.

Reading *New Realms for Writing* reminds me again that, in the end, technology and literacy are intertwined. The technologies of reading and writing (ink, paper, keyboards, screens, and more) have been connected from the beginning of our literate era. Even though the tools change, Michele reminds us that "students must read and write in school with real purpose, think critically, and formulate their own questions." No technology will do that. But, as a teacher, Michele will help you figure out how best to do these things with your own students.

Troy Hicks
Central Michigan University

 # *Introduction*

I was not the strongest student, and I clearly remember sitting at my desk in my bedroom in tears trying to formulate a thesis for an essay assignment for my ninth-grade English class. I couldn't wrap my mind around how to articulate this one sentence, let alone analyze in an essay the book I'd read. Fortunately, my mom sat with me asking questions, writing down what I said, and helping me to craft the essay. She didn't write it for me but encouraged me to put words down on paper without stressing about whether the words sounded right. Writing was difficult for me in high school. Throughout my high school and college years I continued to write more, read a lot, and develop my writing and voice. I will not say that writing became easier, but it did become less painful and more manageable.

Writing is a lifelong skill. The more we write, the better our writing becomes. Fast forward to today: I tell my students of my own obstacles with writing so they might understand that no one is born a great writer. Great writers are made by reading, writing, revising, editing, and writing more.

New Dimensions to Writing

As an eighth-grade English teacher for the past twenty years, I make writing the center of my curriculum. In my classroom, students are working on developing their skills as readers, writers, speakers, listeners, and critical thinkers every day. Whereas my secondary school writing experience consisted of an endless string of essay assignments, today's classrooms offer new possibilities for teaching and supporting our students as writers and creative communicators. Words do not exist only on a page in a two-dimensional space any longer. Today, words are multisensory experiences that are seen, heard, and experienced through podcasting, filmmaking, storytelling, gaming, virtual reality, and design. Writing has evolved in genre, medium, and dimensions. In this day and age, why relegate our students to writing essays? There are so many other possibilities. To help you explore them, *New Realms in Writing* spotlights innovative ways that students can organize, experiment, and demonstrate knowledge construction, understanding, and learning beyond traditional writing assignments.

Teachers have been called upon to empower learners and to bring creativity into educational spaces to promote critical thinking, problem solving, and design thinking while at the same time bolster communication skills. Writing is a key communication skill necessary in school and out to articulate thinking and clarify ideas. Words are powerful; they evoke emotion, persuade people, and contain testimony and history. Shawna Coppola, author of *Renew! Being a Better and More Authentic Writing Teacher* (2017), reminds us "it's important to continually rethink, revise, and renew our practice as teachers of writing" (p. 7). This consists of looking at the ways we use writing for learning input and output. The ISTE Standards for Educators identify educators as leaders and designers who create "authentic learning activities that align with content area standards and use digital tools and resources to maximize active, deep learning" (International Society for Technology in Education [ISTE], 2017).

In the classroom, students write to learn and also write to showcase their learning. Writing to learn consists of short, exploratory, unedited, informal writing opportunities. Public writing is often assessment driven, assigned to demonstrate learning and understanding. It is output driven, planned, drafted, and edited. Public writing consists of essay writing, research reports, creative writing, guidebooks, lab reports, scrapbooks, letters, and presentations. The Common Core State Standards for Literacy address the importance of both content and form to develop students' writing skills. One of the best ways to encourage students to become critical thinkers and strategic learners is to incorporate writing across disciplines. Additionally, the Common Core State Standards place a strong focus on argumentative, informative, and explanatory writing. These standards call for students to become well-rounded individuals who write different types of texts for different purposes and audiences. That means we need to rethink and revise the writing that students create in the classroom to be engaging and authentic and to bring student voice and agency to the forefront.

How This Book Can Help

Technology in education has given carte blanche to writing opportunities by expanding and customizing forms, audience, and products. As the ISTE Standards for Students indicate, technology empowers students as knowledge constructors "to produce creative artifacts and make meaningful learning experiences for themselves and others" (International Society for Technology in Education [ISTE], 2016). Students are able to interact with text and create their own interactive texts in the form of blogs, podcasts, videos, and games. Classroom writing for teaching and learning needs to mirror these real-world texts, "broaden perspectives, and enrich learning through collaborating" (ISTE Standards for Students 7, 2016).

New Realms in Writing is a means for that. Each chapter presents inquiry units across disciplines that focus on writing skills and development while at the same time addressing digital technologies that support and advance student learning. Many of the lessons that are presented throughout the book are aimed at secondary students, but they are adaptable for elementary students and students with diverse needs. Each chapter concludes with a "Key Points" section that discusses the important learning themes from the unit as well as ways to expand the lesson ideas for the students in your classroom. At the end of each chapter, you also will find a table listing resources, links, and technology tools mentioned throughout the chapter to support the writing and learning happening in the classroom. Use this table as a menu to select tools and strategies that will best fit your classroom and student needs. Remember, however, that the menu is always growing as technology evolves. New tools and digital platforms emerge, while others fade out. Always focus on how tools support your teaching objectives; what worked best for me at the time of this writing may be eclipsed by something better by the time you are reading.

And what will you be reading in the chapters ahead?

Chapter One introduces an investigative journalism unit with a concentration in the sciences to answer questions about how the choices we make impact the world. Research and evidence are central to all writing assignments whether informational or argumentative. This chapter explores new alternatives for traditional annotated bibliographies and outlines with updated digital curation tools and infographics. Students write their investigative journalism piece as a culminating project, but extending the project into a podcast is another opportunity to build students' writing and speaking skills.

In Chapter Two, a multigenre interdisciplinary literacy unit about World War II and the Holocaust is explored. Why limit students to one genre per inquiry? More creativity and choice is available when students decide the genres to best convey a message or theme. This chapter first explores combining research with creative writing, then highlights multimedia platforms with which students can create interactive sensory experiences that make words come alive.

Essay writing is still a major part of the secondary schooling experience, and Chapter Three addresses strategies and technology tools, including assistive technology, to help students articulate their thinking in this traditional writing format. Gameboards and HyperDocs are shared to support students through the editing process, providing choice and opportunities to develop their writing skills, grammar, word acquisition, style, and voice.

Chapter Four spotlights poetry and the prospect of students reading, writing, speaking, and hacking poetry. Dabbling with makerspace and coding can make words lift off a page by creating interactive experiences with words. We hear words and see words, so students need to be able to go beyond reading and writing words to produce multisensory experiences that help others to feel and experience the power of words.

In Chapter Five, more maker projects are introduced in conjunction with writing. Writing and making share similar processes when it comes to design thinking. In this chapter, the idea of tinkering is used as a catalyst for writing in addition to a vehicle for writing, reflection, learning, and understanding. The projects presented range from no budget to low budget to big budget. For example, Play-Doh, Lego sets, and recycled materials can be used to articulate thinking or script a creative writing piece. With more costly robotic tools, students can use design thinking and programming to make, as well as writing to record and reflect on the process of making.

Finally, Chapter Six introduces college and career readiness writing for resumes and elevator pitches. Filmmaking, storytelling, and speech writing projects are also presented to enable students to be creative media makers using movie production tools and other digital tools for podcasting and global collaboration. Why should writing in school be tedious or inauthentic? Our students are already immersed in these genres and formats outside of school, so let's bring them into the classroom to help polish students' strengths and skills so they can be creative communicators and compelling writers.

This book is a compilation of lesson ideas that have helped turn my classrooms into an epicenter of creation, communication, and composition. All the lessons presented in the following chapters can be used in isolation, mix and matched, or replicated exactly as I share. You will find teaching activities and lessons that build on student skills and abilities as creative communicators, with suggestions of technology tools to create wider opportunities in an ever-changing digital world.

Whether you use these or your own innovations, strive to use writing to spark authentic and meaningful learning experiences that bring student voice to the forefront and engage your students as stakeholders in their own learning. Our students are creators in their own right as video producers, songwriters, bloggers, gamers, and storytellers. Why not use their strengths to hone in on their writing skills and continue to remix and write new texts with limitless possibilities?

Inquiry-Based Writing

Investigative Science Research, Infographics, Writing, and Podcasting

Our job as educators today is not only to teach content-area skills and knowledge, but also to promote such life skills as creativity, critical thinking, and empathy. Empathy and character education, therefore, are embedded throughout my English curriculum with the books we read and writing students create. I want to help my students develop a social awareness about people and the world around them, so I start the school year with a unit that requires my students to write about their interests and inquiries about the world today. I pose this question to students: What do you wish you could change about your community, your country, your world?

The objectives of this unit are for students to research a topic that interests them and then write an investigative feature article that blends personal narrative writing with research. Grounded in informational nonfiction text, this inquiry-based writing unit requires students to research and write science-based investigative journalism articles, design infographics, and record podcasts with the guiding question: *How do the choices we make impact the world?*

Read, Pair, and Model

English and social studies lend themselves conveniently to reading and writing with historical fiction and written responses for document-based questions (DBQs), but you don't have to limit yourself to just this traditional pairing. Although the majority of my middle-school ELA curriculum is driven by the humanities with such books as *Animal Farm*, *Warriors Don't Cry*, and *To Kill a Mockingbird* on our required eighth-grade reading list, I try to draw in more science connections. For instance, I have incorporated interdisciplinary text pairings between *To Kill a Mockingbird* and articles on rabies from *Using Informational Text* (2014), and, during our Dystopian unit, drew connections between *Animal Farm* and Mark Bittman's editorial "Some Animals Are More Equal Than Others" in *The New York Times*. By making literacy connections between science and English, students can see the interconnectedness between their content-area classes.

When exploring pairings, reach beyond the obvious texts into social sciences, environmental science, biology, psychology, nutrition science and health, earth science and more. With science writers and superstars, such as Mary Roach, Andy Weir, and Neil deGrasse Tyson, and such podcasts as *Science Friday*, *RadioLab*, *Brains On*, and *StarTalk Radio*, science has been brought to the forefront through story. To introduce my students to story-driven science writing, for example, I start with a mentor text and article that addresses environmental science and biology. What better way to engage a middle-school audience than with Mary Beth Grigg's *Popular Science* article, "What Goes into Your Toilet Might Be a Literal Goldmine" (2015)? That's right, I hook them with a poop article, albeit one that discusses precious metals that are found in human excrement. Did you know that the American Chemical Society's intentions are to extract tons of valuable metals from sewage for environmental and financial gain? While the gross factor got my students' attention, the article showed them interesting aspects of how people are trying to change the world by potentially turning recycled human waste into economic gains.

An excellent model to read with students before they attempt their own investigative journalism writing, Grigg's article is an informational text that demonstrates the rhetorical devices of ethos, pathos, and logos (see the sidebar). Used to show credibility, stir emotions, and provide evidence to support one's claims, these rhetorical strategies are the foundations of informative and argumentative writing. As writers, students need to understand how to identify these devices as well as use them to establish credibility so that their readers will trust that their information and reasoning are valid.

In my class, students read nonfiction books independently in conjunction with the inquiry-based writing unit. We do most of our reading and writing in class. Class time includes read-alouds, mini-lessons, independent reading, and writing time. Every day I begin my classes with a read-aloud, whether in the form of audio texts, podcasts, videos, or my own reading of a poem, book excerpt, or essay. The goal is to share an abundance of models and mentors of great, provocative writing so that my students can hear and see strategies to use in their own writing. Sometimes students use these texts as writing

ETHOS, PATHOS, LOGOS

The Greek philosopher Aristotle identified three elements of persuasion—ethos, pathos, and logos—that are commonly used for persuasion, debate, and argument. Students need to be able to identify these rhetorical devices as well as use them for effective communication:

○ **ETHOS** is driven by ethics in the sense of the reputation, values, credibility, and moral character of the author. The writer needs to prove their credibility, as well as appeal to the reader's sense of fairness.

○ **LOGOS** is driven by logic or reason, and ideas are presented in ways that most people find reasonable and convincing. Logos-driven writing contains statistics, facts, or reasons to help readers believe the ideas or arguments are true.

○ **PATHOS** is driven by emotion; the goal is to use language or images that provoke an emotional response in the audience. Emotions can motivate people to believe or act in a certain way.

The New York State Next Generation writing standards imply that students will utilize these rhetorical devices in their own writing. Specifically, Standard 7w states that students should "gather relevant information from multiple sources, access the credibility and accuracy of each source, and investigate the information in writing" (2017). This is the definition of ethos.

prompts, and at other times, the texts serve as discussion starters that coincide with the day's lesson. Where can you find good models? Read articles, listen to podcasts, and watch short videos. Some of my go-to publications include *The New York Times*, *The Atlantic*, *National Geographic*, *WIRED*, and *Mental Floss*. (For my favorite podcasts, see the section "Taking Student Writing Further with Podcasting.") If you want students to write in a specific genre, then you need to immerse them in that style of writing. The world is a text, and as educators we need to be critical readers and writers of all texts: print, digital, visual, and audio. Curriculum is living, not static; it evolves with the times, and texts are added to reflect the changing times. Always be on the lookout for great stories to share with your students.

Researching Ideas: Building Ethos and Logos

For the example inquiry-based writing unit, I want my students to live like science journalists, noticing the world around them and their impact on the world. The daily read-alouds help to build students' world knowledge and introduce subjects that might pique their interest. After we read Mary Grigg's infamous poop article together, for instance, I ask students to write about ideas and aspects that they would like to change in their community or globally. **Figure 1.1** illustrates the organizer that they copy and complete in their English notebooks. After completing the organizer, students share ideas in small groups, then I ask students to narrow down their ideas and select two topics that pique their interest. Then, students spend a class period conducting preliminary research, gathering the Five Ws (who, what, where, when, why) about these topics in their writer's notebooks.

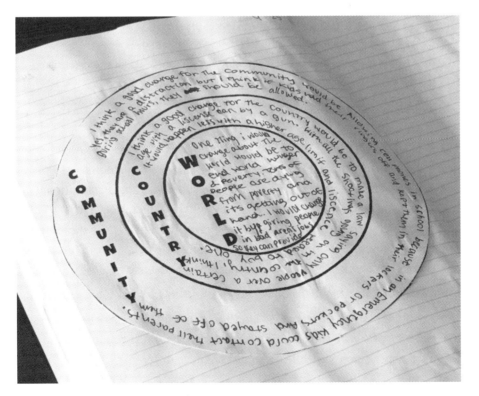

FIGURE 1.1
The "What Do You Wish You Could Change About the World, Country, and Community?" graphic organizer allows students to brainstorm possible topics they want to research and write more about.

Over the course of two class periods, students narrow down their interests and commit to one topic. They then spend more time digging deeper to investigate the topic, gathering information to answer questions they had about their topic, as well as refining and developing more questions. Students spend a week in class reading and researching information that will help them better understand their topic, narrow down their topic, and give their own writing credibility. Based on their research, students then compile an annotated bibliography (see **Figure 1.2**) with four or more reliable and valid sources they used and will reference in their feature article.

FIGURE 1.2
Presenting the Annotated Bibliography Assignment as a checklist helps articulate the requirements and expectations for the completed assignment.

ANNOTATED BIBLIOGRAPHY CHECKLIST

☐ Your annotated bibliography contains four (4) or more citations and annotations.

☐ Citations are in alphabetical order based on the author's last name.

☐ Each annotation contains:

- 3–5 sentences accurately summarizing the article/website
- 3–5 sentences evaluating the credibility and validity of the author/website
- 3–5 sentences explaining how this article/website informs your thinking and will be useful to your own investigative article

☐ You have read through your annotated bibliography, and there are no spelling, grammar, or mechanical issues.

☐ Your font should be consistent throughout the entire document: 12 point font.

The New York State Next Generation Writing Standard W6 requires eighth-grade students to "conduct research to answer questions, including self-generated questions, drawing on multiple sources…generate additional related questions that allow for multiple avenues of exploration" (2017). When students develop their own questions, they have ownership of the topics they are writing about. All writing is grounded in solid research, and when students develop questions and conduct research to help answer those questions they are empowered learners supporting their own learning process.

Not all students learn the same, so some of your students may need additional supports with their writing. Among the scaffolding tools I create to support my students with learning or language differences are graphic organizers to break multistep assignments into bite-size pieces. Graphic organizers are helpful tools for brainstorming, planning, and organizing information before writing or executing a project. This system of support is similar to an outline, breaking down a project into smaller pieces.

Figure 1.3 for example, highlights part of the Annotated Bibliography graphic organizer that I post on for all students in Google Classroom. (To access the full graphic organizer, scan the QR code.) Depending on the students' abilities, you might reduce the quantity of annotations to support their learning needs.

Annotated
Bibliography

DIGITAL CURATION TOOLS: THE 21ST CENTURY ANNOTATED BIBLIOGRAPHY

Creating an annotated bibliography is a traditional secondary school and college assignment, but it's not the only way to manage research resources. Especially for upper-elementary students and early middle-school grades, here are few alternative digital curation tools to help students to be knowledge constructors who collect, annotate, evaluate, and catalog online research that demonstrates "meaningful connections and conclusions" (ISTE Standards for Students, 3c, 2016):

○ **DIIGO** is a digital bookmarking tool that enables students to bookmark resources and websites, as well as add notes and annotations. With Diigo, students can highlight an important quote on a web page and share their notes and annotations with others.

○ **GOOGLE KEEP** allows students to add web resources into their Google Keep Notepad and curate their own resources.

○ **LIVEBINDERS** allow students to create virtual notebooks to house their research and web sources.

○ **PINTEREST** is a visual bookmarking tool where students save "pins" onto their virtual boards (think digital bulletin board). Students can create their own boards to curate their resources, including websites, articles, videos, and even Google files.

○ **SYMBALOOEDU** lets students store online resources as Symbaloo Webmixes, which are virtual boards (similar to Pinterest) that students can color code, and label their favorite sites, videos, and digital files.

○ **THINGLINK** lets students create interactive infographics to link resources and web content together in one place.

○ **WEBJETS** is another curation tool that allows students to bookmark, list, and create tables and grids for content collected from the web into interactive notecards.

SAMPLE ANNOTATION

Schwartz, J. (2016, February 26). Decline of pollinators poses threat to world food supply, report says. *The New York Times*. Retrieved from https://www.nytimes.com/2016/02/27/science/decline-of-species-that-pollinate-poses-a-threat-to-global-food-supply-report-warns.html

In this article from *The New York Times*, author John Schwartz describes the threat of extinction of bees, birds, and bats due to climate change, aggressive agricultural practices, and genetically modified organisms. This article offers multiple reasons for the decline in pollinating animals and insects. Human interaction affects animal survival, and there is an interdependent relationship between people and insects. Bees and birds are necessary to help pollinate flowers, fruits, vegetables, and nuts. As a result, these species help pollinate and support our food supply. Schwartz is a contributor to *The New York Times* with a focus on climate change. The article cites a United Nations report, making this article informative and trustworthy. Although there are no solutions presented in the article, it is clear on the causes of the extinction of these animals and insects. I can use this information for credibility and because it contains several relevant arguments I can bring attention to in my own article on what is happening to the bee population.

- Citation in APA Format.
- States the source and the author and summarizes the article.
- Evaluates the credibility of the author and his/her research.
- Explains how the article informs thinking and writing.

CITATION	
citationmachine.net	
SUMMARY	
What is the website or article about?	
ETHOS	
Describe the credibility of the author or website. What makes them reliable and trustworthy?	
INFORMING	
Describe how this article or website informs your thinking and will be useful to your own investigative journalism article.	

For a copy of this graphic organizer with space for additional annotations go to theteachingfactor.com

FIGURE 1.3 The Annotated Bibliography Graphic Organizer breaks down the elements of an annotation so students do not only summarize their research findings, but also address the validity of the source and how it informs their own thinking and writing.

The annotated bibliography is the foundation of the students' investigative writing. It catalogs their research and findings. Finding valid and reliable (ethos) information in the form of facts, statistics, and testimony (logos) helps inform and persuade. Evidence includes testimony, statistics, facts, and examples. Students are encouraged to collect quotes and testimony from experts and credible sources. This lends itself to an important mini-lesson on identifying credible and reliable sources. Your school librarian or media specialist is a great person to seek out and help prepare this lesson for your students. Your school might already have databases with websites and research articles from credible authors, journalists, and writers for students to utilize. Citation websites such as BibMe, KnightCite, and CitationMachine help students properly cite each text. Once students have the research and logos to support their topic, it is time to put together the story they are going to write about that topic.

Outlining and Infographics

Writing is a process. I have yet to meet a writer who sits down at the computer and is able to write an entire book, poem, article, or screenplay in one sitting. Writing requires planning, research, writing, revising, rereading, and then writing and revising some more. It also has to start somewhere, and staring at a blank page can be daunting, especially for students. The challenge is to take their notes and turn them into a written piece that expresses their ideas. Outlines are useful writing tools for getting ideas down on paper in this prewriting stage, as are infographics.

An infographic is a visually appealing document that is used to represent data or information with words, graphs, images, and numbers. Like an outline, it strips down content to the main idea and supporting details. When students create an infographic, they have to synthesize the information they curated and make meaning for others by presenting their information is a way that stands out and is easy to read. Using such tools as Canva, Piktochart, Buncee, and Google Drawings, students can design an infographic that visually communicates the key information gathered from their research. In Google Drawings, students are starting with a blank page;

in Canva, Buncee, and Piktochart, students can choose a template to personalize by adding data and graphics based on their research and information.

Before your students create their own infographics, encourage them to look at many examples of infographics to examine the ways that information is presented, the use of color, and the balance between image and text, and then to keep these aspects in mind when creating their own infographic. The structure and format of the data should be based on the structure of their investigative piece: compare and contrast, cause and effect, or problem and solution. The text structures of an infographic (how the author organizes information and presents main ideas in the text) are similar to the text structures of any nonfiction text. Visual.ly has a great gallery of infographics that contains useful examples for showing to students.

Having students visually represent their data in an infographic requires them to choose words and images purposefully in order to communicate an idea, prove their thinking, and possibly persuade their viewers. Students meet Common Core State Standards because they are translating "quantitative or technical information expressed in words in a text into visual form (e.g., a table or chart)" and translating "information expressed visually or mathematically (e.g., in an equation) into words" (CCSS.ELA-Literacy.RST.9-10.7). Additionally, students are making "strategic use of digital media and visual displays of data to express information and enhance understanding of presentations" (CCSS.ELA-Literacy.CCRA.SL.5). At a time when information is represented in words, information, numbers, and graphs, having students read and represent these many formats builds on their creative communication skills. By creating infographics, students are also acting as empowered learners (ISTE Standards for Students 1c, 2016), using technology to demonstrate their learning through graphic design. **Figure 1.4** presents a student-created infographic that helped her outline her research and write her feature article.

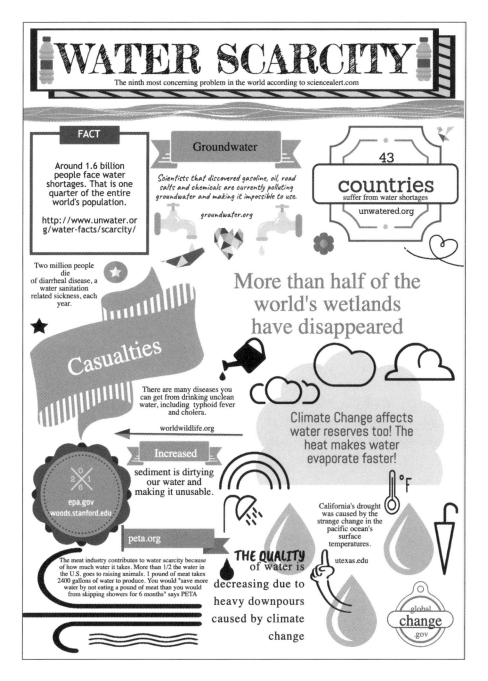

FIGURE 1.4
Using Piktochart, a student created this infographic during the prewriting stage for an article on water scarcity.

Let's Write: Crafting a Lede

Once the research is complete and the outlines are done, it is time for your students to begin transforming their new knowledge and understanding into a journalistic-style article that blends information, personal narrative, and maybe some persuasion with ethos, pathos, and logos.

As readers, we know that beginnings are important. Called a *lede* (sometimes spelled *lead*), the beginning of a writing piece has to hook the reader and draw them into the text. In the first few sentences, writers need to craft an opening that will capture the reader's attention and at the same time evoke a response to the topic. Journalist Jenna Fisher did this effectively in an article for the *Christian Science Monitor* (2013), writing:

> *Tom McNichol has fished a lot of strange things out of Boston's Charles River. Among the most unexpected are a portable toilet, a recliner, and a dead body.*

Fisher's lede is intriguing and descriptive, plus it has a surprise element. Readers are immediately drawn into her writing because she uses vivid examples of "strange things." In my classroom, Fisher's example helps start a discussion on effective ledes in journalism. During a mini-lesson, students are introduced to five lede strategies to try out in their own writing (**Figure 1.5**). Looking at many examples from popular magazines and newspapers, students deconstruct their opening lines, examining sentence structure and word choice to understand the craft of writing, while at the same time thinking of effective ledes for their own writing. Modeling different ledes helps students select a style that fits with the objective of their article and borrow writing strategies from the pros.

If we want our students to write engaging and beautifully crafted pieces, we need to immerse them in great writing and allow them time to write during class every day. In their book *180 Days: Two Teachers and the Quest to Engage and Empower Adolescents* (2018), Kelly Gallagher and Penny Kittle wrote, "make sure the quality of the writing you share inspires students to write well. Write alongside your students and share writing and thinking

"THE LEDE"

Journalists begin stories with what is called a **"lede."** Ledes are the foundation of every news story. A strong lede informs, invites, and tempts the reader. It is critical to whether the reader is willing to invest time in a story.

Question Lede	Pose a rhetorical question to your readers.	Humanity began in Africa. But we didn't stay there, not all of us—over thousands of years our ancestors walked all over the continent, then out of it. And when they came to the sea, they built boats and sailed tremendous distances to islands they could not have known were there. Why?	**The 12 Greatest Challenges for Space Exploration** *WIRED* 02.16.16
Teaser Lede	Use one word or phrase as a teaser throughout your lede.	Everybody poops, as you may have read, and people in space are no exception. In zero gravity, astronauts rely on vacuum-powered toilets to help get feces far away from the body. Once it's shot out of the space station, astronaut poop burns up in the atmosphere like shooting stars, which is cool and great.	**NASA Wants You (Yes, You) to Solve Its Poop Problems** By Rachel Feltman *Popular Science* 11.28.16
Summary Lede	Include the Five Ws and H in your lede: Who? What? Where? When? Why? How?	We have shot, hanged, gassed, electrocuted, and lethally injected hundreds of people to carry out legally sanctioned executions. Thousands more await their execution on death row.	***Just Mercy: A Story of Justice and Redemption*** By Bryan Stevenson 2015
Descriptive Lede	Use descriptive language and vivid imagery to draw the reader in and create a picture in the mind's eye.	I grabbed my coat and ran down the marble stairs, passing construction workers, and hurried onto Chambers St. Sirens were now splitting the air and there were police lines being set up on Broadway. Several hundred New Yorkers were on the north side of the street gazing up at the World Trade Center. A great gray cloud billowed in slow motion, growing larger and larger, like some evil genie released into the cloudless sky. Twisted hunks of metal were falling off the ruined facade. Sheets of paper fluttered against the grayness like ghostly snowflakes.	**Death Takes Hold Among the Living After 9/11 Attack** By Pete Hamill *The New York Daily News* 09.12.01
Contrast Lede	Use contrasting images or anecdote to illustrate the point of the story.	Eight miles off the coast of Long Beach, CA, the oil rig Eureka, which has stood here for 40 years, is a study in contrasts. From a distance, it looks just like another offshore platform, an artifact of the modern industrial landscape. But beneath the waves, the Eureka, and other rigs like it in the area are home to a vast and thriving community of sea life that some scientists say is one of the richest marine ecosystems on the planet.	**Marine Life Thrives in Unlikely Places: Offshore Oil Rigs** By Erik Olsen *The New York Times* 03.07.16

FIGURE 1.5 As part of a mini-lesson, I provide students with examples of five lede strategies to hook readers.

about revision" (p. 39). These writing models and mentors also are helpful for mini-lessons about craft and the evolution of the writing process.

Beyond great writing examples, I also give my students a Lede Passport (see **Figure 1.6**) to encourage them to try out crafting different types of ledes for the opening sentences of their feature article. For a game element, have students roll a dice and based on the number they roll, try out that type of lede on the graphic organizer in Figure 1.6. When working with this activity, I allow enough time for each student to try two or three types of ledes.

FIGURE 1.6
To challenge students to try different opening strategies, turn it into a game: Roll the dice, and try a lede type based on the resulting number.

LEDE PASSPORT: ROLL THE DICE & SEE WHICH LEDES TO WRITE.	
Directions: Roll the dice, and write a lede for the number the dice lands on. Collect a stamp for each lede that you write out. Key: *(1) Question Lede; (2) Teaser Lede; (3) Summary Lede; (4) Descriptive Lede; (5) Contrast Lede*	
Lede #1 Strategy:	
Lede #2 Strategy:	
Lede #3 Strategy:	

Lily's Article

During this exercise, Lily wrote the following lede, which uses a list format to introduce mass school shootings. She also uses a rhetorical question in her article's opening to draw readers into the problem and solution it presents. Scan the QR code to read Lily's investigative journalism article on school shootings in its entirety.

April 20, 1999, Columbine High School in Littleton, Colorado:
15 dead and 24 injured.

December 14, 2012, Sandy Hook Elementary School in Newtown, Connecticut:
20 first graders and six adults killed.

October 1, 2017, Route 91 Harvest music festival in Las Vegas, Nevada:
59 people killed and 851 injured.

February 14, 2018, Stoneman Douglas High School in Parkland, Florida:,
7 people killed and 17 injured.

Should I keep going?

Ledes invite readers into one's writing and often introduce a topic. Continuously offering models and sentence stems for students to borrow and make their own helps student writers experiment and stretch their writing muscles, while at the same time boosts vocabulary and builds word knowledge.

Blending Personal Narrative and Research

Because the investigative feature article for the inquiry-based unit blends personal narrative writing with research, students can pursue topics that personally impact them, their families, or their interests. According to Kelly Gallagher, author of *In the Best Interest of Students* (2015), personal experience can strengthen an argument, and including a personal story or story element builds pathos and helps readers connect on an emotional level with the information. For many of my students, for example, our first lockdown drill stirred emotion and conversations about school shootings. A handful of students later chose to research school shootings and gun control laws for this assignment.

Weaving personal stories and research into a cohesive article requires blending ideas, facts, testimony, and story. Stories weave into and out of the research. If their topic did not have a personal connection, students found stories that would help appeal to the reader's emotions. These stories were in the form of testimony and quoted words. During our writing workshop, I modeled blending personal story with informational data in my own writing, sometimes using a document camera or by projecting Google Docs on a SMARTBoard. My intention in modeling my writing process was to create a dialogue about the writing process rather than simply telling students "this is how it's done." I wanted to show students my thinking, edits, and revisions in crafting a piece. Showing my vulnerability as a writer helped students to see that writing is a process and a work in progress until the due date.

Surprisingly, many of my students felt comfortable writing about very personal topics, and I was impressed by the honesty in their writing. I learned so much about my students by working on this unit because of the stories they shared through their writing. Kate's essay about her struggles as a cancer survivor and how chemotherapy can be as harmful as helpful (**Figure 1.7**) was one of the most powerful and poignant I have received to this day.

When topics are personal, they are powerful, and the articles written for this unit are frequently some of the strongest writing presented the entire school year. In her book *The Journey Is Everything* (2016), Katherine Bomer called for reclaiming the essay from being a watered-down, rote five paragraphs driven by a "bossy, single sentence"—the dreaded thesis (p. 31). She argued students need the freedom to explore topics about everything, driven by "curiosity, passion, and the intricacies of thought" (p. 33). I agree with Bomer: Teachers need to reclaim writing and enable students to write about topics that pique their interests, draw upon personal connections, and allow them to discover who they are and who they want to be.

CHEMOTHERAPY—DESTROYING OR SAVING LIVES?

By Kate S.

Most people would say that getting cancer as a child is rare. But if you put it this way, your chances of winning the lottery, 1 in 175,000,000. The chances of a child getting cancer, 1 in 285. So, it's not rare. And unfortunately I was that one child, the 1 out of 285, who was diagnosed with cancer when I was only 5 years old.

When my family and I received the news that AML (acute monocytic leukemia) had officially taken over my body, we really were up for any treatment options, even options that would damage my body forever. And with an overall survival rate of 25%, my parents realized that I needed treatment immediately. They didn't really care what the treatment was, as long as it would treat the cancer and hopefully save my life.

Most people who are given the news that they have cancer have many different treatment options all depending on the type of cancer they have. Radiation, surgery, immunotherapy, stem cell transplant, transfusions can all be used to treat cancer but the most commonly used, for almost all cancers, is Chemotherapy.

For me, my cancer treatment plan consisted of chemotherapy, but when that didn't help much, my doctors decided a Bone Marrow Transplant would be my best chance for survival. The Bone Marrow Transplant that I received from my little sister on November 14th, 2007, did in fact cure me and here I am now living a cancer free life 8 years later.

Most patients, when told they have cancer are not worried about what Chemotherapy will do to them in the future, but more about the hair loss, vomiting, reduced immunity, and of course the fear of death. At the time, hair loss seemed to be my only worry but little did I know the long term effects that I experience now unquestionably outweigh the once devastating baldness.

The long term side effects of Chemotherapy really have only been researched within the past couple of years, so when I was diagnosed in 2007, my family wasn't thoroughly informed of the dangers that could possibly happen in years to come. And even if doctors knew about the permanent side effects, most patients would realize that they are in a life or death situation and would be eager to try anything that might help them live.

Dr. Deborah Schrag, graduate of Harvard Medical School and oncologist at the Dana–Farber Cancer Institute in Boston states "according to the study, 2/3 of people with advanced cancer believe going through chemotherapy might cure them, even though their doctors are well aware that the odds are it will do no such thing."

Once chemotherapy is injected into your body through IVs or pills, it targets cancer cells to slow the growth. But as research shows, it will target healthy cells as well, and the damage it does to the healthy cells is what causes the short term side effects that consist of constant vomiting, hair-loss, reduced immunity, and anemia. All which may cause emotional distress to some patients but chemotherapy also leaves behind the long-term or permanent side effects of organ damage, heart damage, infertility, Endocrine (hormone) system damage, Brain/Spinal cord/nerve damage, learning difficulties and secondary cancers.

Growing up with cancer took my childhood away, and even though the short term side effects may have upset me then, it's the organ damage, heart weakness, Endocrine System damage, and infertility that I suffer with now that leaves me in awe today. But over the years I've come to realize that as a cancer survivor, I would much rather be here on earth suffering with these permanent side effects than have died 8 years ago.

And all of this recent research truly reveals that chemotherapy, the drug once thought to save your life, might actually hurt you.

But what is the alternative then? Chemotherapy has been used to treat cancer since the 1950s and most scientists are now realizing it's time for an update.

Dr. Vijay Chudasama, for the last 5 years has been working on another procedure to eliminate the need for chemotherapy. This new procedure would be able to distinguish the difference between cancerous tissue and healthy tissue, which would be a huge improvement for cancer research because the terrible side effects, both short term and long term, from chemotherapy would be eliminated.

So chances are, at least once in your lifetime, you will know someone that has been diagnosed with cancer and needs treatment immediately. And there's a good chance they will undergo chemotherapy at least once in their cancer career.

So it's our job to inform these patients what chemotherapy could do to them and if they are willing to take this risk. No fourteen year old girl should have to worry about her organ damage, heart weakness, Hormone deficiency, infertility, and the recurring nightmare that the cancer will come back. This is what chemotherapy left her with over 8 years ago.

So talk to your doctor and make sure you know your options and what could potentially happen if you receive chemotherapy. And always remember there are other alternatives, and hopefully soon there will be no more need for this toxic drug.

FIGURE 1.7 In this science-based feature article, a student wove personal narrative and research into a powerful piece.

Taking Student Writing Further with Podcasting

Students' personal stories and investigative journalism articles do not have to end with their submitted writing pieces. Whereas writing is visual, podcasting brings in an audio element that reaches a wider audience. Podcasts are an effective medium to share knowledge and experiences, and students can easily create their own. You could introduce podcasting during the inquiry unit as a side quest, an extra credit opportunity for students, or an extension of the unit by having students revise their writing into an engaging podcast. Podcasting with students improves literacy skills, creates an authentic audience for writing, and develops writing with revision and attention to audience. I not only use podcasts as texts to read closely and critically with students, I also expanded the inquiry unit for students to write and record their own podcasts in the style of National Public Radio's *RadioLab*. (For a complete discussion of the unit, see "Building Literacy *RadioLab* Style: Podcasting to Foster Speech and Debate Skills," a chapter I wrote for Mark Gura's *Teaching Literacy in the Digital Age* (ISTE, 2014).)

Hosted by Jad Abumrad and Robert Krulwich, *RadioLab* combines reporting and documentary on topics from science to philosophy. In essence, the podcast is presented as a five-paragraph informative essay about specific scientific inquiries: The podcasts all begin with a hook to invite the listener in and then introduce the topic or theme for the show; this first three to five minutes is similar to an introductory paragraph. Then, the hosts present the "body paragraphs": their evidence and stories to expand the understanding of the topic for the listener. To conclude, the hosts reflect aloud and allow the listeners to make their own decisions about the information presented. The engaging parts of *RadioLab* are not only the stories themselves, but the way the hosts present the materials with sound effects, interview excerpts (testimony), and a conversational style.

RadioLab is one style of podcasting, but students can also listen to models of podcasts that take a question-and-answer, educational, and even theater approach. To complement the inquiry-based article, you can find many great science-based podcasts, from Neil deGrasse Tyson's *StarTalk Radio* to

Dick Gordon's *The Story*. How you want students to present their podcasts is a decision that you and your students have to make. Maybe offer choices. By offering students choices there will be a diversity of products, students will have agency, and their voices will be at the forefront of their finished products. A podcast assignment allows students to be creative communicators who "select and use digital tools to plan and manage a design process that considers design constraints and calculated risks" (ISTE Standards for Students 4b, 2016). Students "publish or present content that customizes the message and medium for their intended audiences" (ISTE Standards for Students 6d, 2016).

Building strong communication skills, both verbally and in writing, requires students to revise their writing and adjust it according to the intended audience once the format and style are selected. When podcasting, students are not just reading aloud their writing but carefully choosing sound effects, recording interviews, and including sound bites from experts, adding engaging features that draw the listener's attention. As the creators of *Lethal Lit: A Tig Torres Mystery* podcast series Alex Segura and Monica Gallagher stated in an interview, "With audio, you have to drop clues and be a bit more literal. You can only rely on the audio. There's no picture or caption to guide things along. So it all has to be there in the narration and dialogue, which puts a huge focus on how the characters talk, how the show is produced and the pacing" (2018). With podcasts, it is about making the story engaging for listeners.

To create their podcasts, students can use a variety of tools. Audacity, GarageBand, and Soundtrap are three good choices for recording their podcasts. Audacity is a free online tool that allows you to record and edit digital files. GarageBand is an app for Macs and iOS mobile devices that enables you to create sound files and edit sound files. Part of G Suite for Google EDU Schools, Soundtrap offers recording and editing. To add interesting sound effects to podcasts, students can download Creative Commons Licensed sounds from the Freesound database. Students can also use screencast platforms such as Screencastify or Screencast-O-Matic.

When creating podcasts, both teachers and students need to think about the objective for creating the podcast. Will you be grading students on the podcast, and if so, what elements are you grading? Make sure to have

examples and models for students to study and borrow from to build their own podcast. In addition, think about how much revision from the original assignment students will have to do and what graphic organizers or scaffolding you will need to have on hand to help your students succeed.

Key Points

The inquiry-based unit is driven by student choice and engagement. The topics that students write and podcast about are personal to them, and the assignments presented in this chapter help students build on their ideas and thinking. In this unit, I favor a science connection, but you can adapt any of the activities for any subject area. Students might create infographics on the impact of a particular war on the society, politics, and economics of a region or country. Or, students can collaborate by writing and producing a podcasting series based on Sean Carroll's "What Would Stephen Hawking Do?" episode of *The Story Collider*. You could even switch the theme to "What Would Our Founding Fathers Do?" regarding current political issues of contention. For example, a group of students could research, write, and podcast what Abraham Lincoln would do about school shootings and gun laws, while another group addressed how Alexander Hamilton would handle the illegal immigration debate.

TABLE 1.1 **Tools, Strategies, and Standards**

Teaching Techniques & Strategies	Resources	Links	ISTE Standards for Students	Common Core State Standards
Science Writing	*Brains On*	brainson.org	3d. Knowledge Constructor	CCSS.ELA-Literacy.RI.9-10.3
	Mental Floss	mentalfloss.com	Students build knowledge by actively exploring real-world issues and problems, developing ideas and theories and pursuing answers and solutions.	Analyze how the author unfolds an analysis or series of ideas or events, including the order in which the points are made, how they are introduced and developed, and the connections that are drawn between them.
	National Geographic	nationalgeographic.com		
	The New York Times	nytimes.com		
	Science Friday	sciencefriday.com/listen		
	Science Times	nytimes.com/section/science		
	StarTalk Radio	startalkradio.net		
	"What Goes into Your Toilet Might Be a Literal Goldmine" (Grigg, *Popular Science*, 2015)	goo.gl/4BfvYF		
	WIRED	wired.com		
Annotated Bibliography	BibMe	bibme.org	3c. Knowledge Constructor	CCSS.ELA-Literacy.W.8.1
	Citation Machine	citationmachine.net	Students curate information from digital resources using a variety of tools and methods to create collections of artifacts that demonstrate meaningful connections or conclusions.	Write arguments to support claims with clear reasons and relevant evidence.
	KnightCite	calvin.edu/library/knightcite		CCSS.ELA-Literacy.W.8.2
	ZoteroBib	zbib.org		Write informative/ explanatory texts to examine a topic and convey ideas, concepts, and information through the selection, organization, and analysis of relevant content.
Digital Curation Tools	Diigo	diigo.com	3c. Knowledge Constructor	CCSS.ELA-Literacy.RI.9-10.1
	Google Keep	keep.google.com	Students curate information from digital resources using a variety of tools and methods to create collections of artifacts that demonstrate meaningful connections or conclusions.	Cite strong and thorough textual evidence to support analysis of what the text says explicitly as well as inferences drawn from the text.
	LiveBinders	livebinders.com		
	Pinterest	pinterest.com		
	SymbalooEDU	edu.symbaloo.com		
	ThingLink	thinglink.com/edu		
	Webjets	webjets.io		

continued

Teaching Techniques & Strategies	Resources	Links	ISTE Standards for Students	Common Core State Standards
Infographics	Buncee Canva Google Drawings Piktochart Visual.ly Gallery	edu.buncee.com canva.com docs.google.com/drawings piktochart.com visual.ly/view	**4b. Innovative Designer** Students select and use digital tools to plan and manage a design process that considers design constraints and calculated risks. **6b. Creative Communicator** Students create original works or responsibly repurpose or remix digital resources into new creations.	CCSS.ELA-Literacy. RST.9-10.7 Translate quantitative or technical information expressed in words in a text into visual form (e.g., a table or chart) and translate information expressed visually or mathematically (e.g., in an equation) into words. CCSS.ELA-Literacy. SL.9-10.5 Make strategic use of digital media (e.g., textual, graphical, audio, visual, and interactive elements) in presentations to enhance understanding of findings, reasoning, and evidence and to add interest.
Blending Story and Research	*The Story Collider*	storycollider.org	**6c. Creative Communicator** Students communicate complex ideas clearly and effectively by creating or using a variety of digital objects such as visualizations, models or simulations.	CCSS.ELA-Literacy.W.8.1 Write arguments to support claims with clear reasons and relevant evidence CCSS.ELA-Literacy.W.8.2 Write informative/ explanatory texts to examine a topic and convey ideas, concepts, and information through the selection, organization, and analysis of relevant content.
Podcasting	Audacity Freesound GarageBand *Lethal Lit: A Tig Torres Mystery* Pro-Ject Audio *RadioLab* Screencast-O-Matic Screencastify Soundtrap *StarTalk Radio* *The Story* "What Would Stephen Hawking Do?" (Carroll, *The Story Collider*, 2015)	audacityteam.com freesound.org apple.com/mac/garageband tigtorres.com project-audio.com radiolab.org screencast-o-matic.com screencastify.com soundtrap.com startalkradio.net thestory.org goo.gl/fSh7tm	**6c. Creative Communicator** Students communicate complex ideas clearly and effectively by creating or using a variety of digital objects such as visualizations, models or simulations. **6b. Creative Communicator** Students create original works or responsibly repurpose or remix digital resources into new creations.	CCSS.ELA-Literacy.W.8.2 Write informative/ explanatory texts to examine a topic and convey ideas, concepts, and information through the selection, organization, and analysis of relevant content. CCSS.ELA-Literacy. SL.9-10.5 Make strategic use of digital media (e.g., textual, graphical, audio, visual, and interactive elements) in presentations to enhance understanding of findings, reasoning, and evidence and to add interest.

Multigenre Writing

Blending English and Social Studies to Examine the Holocaust and World War II

Why just box students into writing one genre per unit? There are limitations to teaching narrative, informative, and argumentative writing in isolation. Each genre has its strengths and drawbacks. In fact, when we read essays and articles, these genres are often blended together. If teachers allow students to show their understanding and knowledge of a topic with a variety of types of writing, there is opportunity for choice and creativity. This goes beyond just allowing students to choose a genre or format to showcase their understanding. What if students could blend genres across one writing assignment to produce a multigenre piece that includes poetry, narrative, images, songs, and historical fiction to reveal information about their topic?

In a multigenre project, writers consciously select genres and words to convey theme, tone, and point of view. Author of *Blending Genres, Altering Styles*, Tom Romano explained that

> *multigenre projects entail a series of generic documents that are linked by a central premise, theme, or goal. They may forward an argument, trace a history, or offer multiple interpretations of a text or event. They are rigorous forms of writing, involving all of the elements of a traditional research paper: research and citation, coherence and organization, purpose and aim of discourse, audience awareness, and conventional appropriateness. (2000, p. xi)*

Writing is a means of expression that allows a person to respond and reflect on important concepts and ideas. Whereas in Chapter One I focused on using writing as a vehicle for cross-disciplinary writing between English and science, in this chapter I focus on blending English with the humanities. Specifically, I will detail an interdisciplinary project between English and social studies that focuses on the Holocaust and World War II. The writing that students produce during this unit is grounded in research and primary sources. Through innovative and creative writing, students showcase their critical thinking, analysis, and synthesis of the events in history. Students choose from multiple genres—including but not limited to poetry, essays, personal narratives, art, diary entries, and letters—to present a unifying theme communicating the challenges during this time. You will also learn about digital publishing tools students can use to share their writing with a wider audience and become global communicators and collaborators.

Blending English and History

English and social studies lend themselves well to collaborating content and literacy skills, and the World War II era offers an abundance of materials for the classroom beyond textbooks. There are so many wonderful reading choices—historical novels, poetry, and nonfiction—about this time period that might already be in your English curriculum. Or, perhaps you're using primary documents, photographs, films, and documentaries to teach the history of this era. If we want our students to become critical citizens who participate in civic and digital life in positive ways, learning has to be driven by inquiry rather than rote memorization of facts. The new C3 Framework for Social Studies State Standards and the Common Core State Standards for Literacy both support this by advocating critical thinking and close reading of these diverse texts to promote understanding.

In planning the collaborative unit, I worked with my colleague and social studies teacher Francesca Miller, whose teaching philosophy requires her students to reflect on how choices impact outcomes. Her students study primary documents to understand, think critically, and reflect on history and its influence on our world today. We had collaborated previously during our monthly Twitter book chats, combining historical fiction with study of related time periods. (For more detail, see Chapter 4 of *Personalized Reading.*) For this multigenre writing unit, our rationale was to assist students in developing an understanding of the roots and ramifications of prejudice, racism, and stereotyping in any society.

We started with the end project in mind, thinking how we might create an opportunity for creative fiction combined with writing grounded in history and primary sources. We decided for the culmination of this unit students would highlight a common theme prevalent in World War II by creating a multigenre project that incorporated five creative fiction texts, each supported by specific historical documents. The purpose of this project was for students to develop research skills, strengthen writing skills, review how to document sources, and explore writing in multiple genres. Students would need to use higher order thinking and comprehension skills, while at the same time using 21st century skills as digital citizens and creators.

Reading: A Doorway to Writing

Allowing students to analyze, synthesize, and evaluate historical text (primary and secondary sources) across a multitude of texts, genres, and formats allows them to see the depth of history and personal accounts. A textbook alone cannot do this justice. History is more than one text or voice. Introducing multiple voices, texts, and perspectives builds empathy and understanding that history is living and breathing. With this in mind, I used Alexandra Zapruder's *Salvaged Pages: Young Writers' Diaries of the Holocaust* as an entry point for teaching about the Holocaust in my English classroom. The diary entries collected in *Salvaged Pages* are primary documents, first-person accounts from young people who witnessed the atrocities leading up the Holocaust. Many of the diary entries are of young teens writing about Jewish neighbors and family members being sent to the ghettos and concentration camps. In the study guide to the documentary film *I'm Still Here: Real Diaries of Young People who Lived During the Holocaust* (2005), which was based on *Salvaged Pages*, Zapruder wrote in a letter to the reader about these teen diarists,

> They shed light on the historical reality of a moment that is past, and they capture for perennial contemplation the conundrum of life and its meaning in the context of suffering, deprivation, and despair. They do not offer easy answers or tidy summaries. To the contrary, their richness lies in the contradictions and struggles that young writers voiced as they traversed an alien and unfamiliar terrain. Perhaps most important of all, they stand as markers of people in time, those who wrote themselves into existence when the world was trying to erase their presence. (pg. 6)

Working with these diary entries, students learned about this period in history through the eyes of a young person similar of age. The diary entries are powerful as standalone text, and you could have students write in response to the various diary entries. I chose to use a guided discussion technique and differentiated activity to have students reflect, synthesize, and make connections after students read multiple diary entries. Taking turns in small groups, students rolled a dice, then answered the Think Dot discussion question that correlated with the number rolled (**Figure 2.1**). You can use Think Dots as a discussion tool or for written responses.

FIGURE 2.1
A differentiated activity like this Think Dots activity can be used for student writing prompts or to initiate small group discussions after reading historical documents.

Complete the **Think Dots Activity:** Each person at your table will take turns rolling the dice and complete the learning task from the corresponding dot.

What does this diary tell you about living in this state, country, in this year?	How does this diary writer feel? How might the letter recipient feel?
What does it tell you about this teenager and his life? What is this person concerned, worried, or struggling with?	What conclusions can I draw from this diary about this time period?
How do different forms of self-expression communicate different information, observations, and feelings?	If you are writing for yourself, or for comfort, or for other personal reasons, does it matter how well you write? Where does literary talent or skill come into play here? Does the beauty of the language or the literary expressiveness matter in this context?
If you roll TWO ODDs in a row . . . Choose several words or phrases from the entries that capture important historical information from the diary. What words or phrases convey emotions? What passages stand out?	If you roll TWO EVENs in a row . . . How do different forms of self-expression communicate different information, observations, and feelings?

HOLOCAUST RESOURCES

The nonprofit, international organization Facing History is an excellent source of material for multigenre units. Facing History creates curriculum and produces professional development on issues of racism, prejudice, and antisemitism. The mission of Facing History is "to engage students of diverse backgrounds in an examination of racism, prejudice, and anti-Semitism in order to promote the development of a more humane and informed citizenry" (n.d.). The resources and materials that Facing History has curated include primary sources, multimedia materials, historical fiction, lesson plans, and full units (including one on *Salvaged Pages*) available online.

Don't stop with diaries: You can find a variety of formats to meet all readers' needs—narrative, memoir, graphic novels, vignettes, and historical fiction. In my English class, students participated in book clubs and chose from a selection of young adult books about World War II and the Holocaust. The independent reading and book club discussions coincided with the history lessons that students were learning in their social studies class. (For recommendations of a variety of books about World War II and the Holocaust that range in text type and reading levels, see the sidebar "Reading Recommendations." For lesson plans, supplementary texts, videos, and more on the Holocaust, see the sidebar "Holocaust Resources.")

My class even practiced close reading of visual texts by studying paintings by artists that Hitler labeled as "degenerate." Using visual thinking strategies, they closely examined the images painted and the expressions conveyed by such artists as George Grosz, Ernst Ludwig Kirchner, Paul Klee, Georg Kolbe, Wilhelm Lehmbruck, Franz Marc, Emil Nolde, Otto Dix, and others. Students closely viewed the color, subjects, and lighting in the artwork, and many were inspired to create their own drawings and paintings in response to the events they read about.

While students are learning about history's key events in their social studies classes, they can be reading about survivors, resistors, upstanders, and true events depicted in the book club books they choose. Reading these books while writing helps to build understanding of this period in history, as well as study the craft and writing styles presented in the text. Encourage your

READING RECOMMENDATIONS

Sorting through the volume of literature and nonfiction written about World War II can be a daunting task. To help you, here are some that my students and I enjoy.

NONFICTION & MEMOIR

The Diary of Anne Frank by Anne Frank

Irena's Children by Tilar Mazzeo

The Boys Who Challenged Hitler by Phillip Hoose

Farewell to Manzanar by Jeanne Wakatsuki Houston and James D. Houston

Night by Eli Wiesel

Upon the Head of the Goat by Aranka Siegal

HISTORICAL FICTION

Refugee by Alan Gratz

Between Shades of Gray by Ruta Sepetys

Salt to the Sea by Ruta Sepetys

The Librarian of Auschwitz by Antonio Iturbe

Lily's Crossing by Patricia Reilly Giff

Number the Stars by Lois Lowry

Someday We Will Fly by Rachel Dewoskin

White Rose by Kip Wilson

GRAPHIC NOVELS

Maus I & Maus II by Art Spiegelman

Resistance: Book 1 by Carla Jablonski and Leland Purvis

Good-bye Marianne by Irene N. Watts and Kathryn E. Shoemaker

students to not simply read for information, but also to read like writers. When students met in their book clubs in my classroom, for example, they discussed the events taking place in their readings, and then I would ask them to look at specific writerly intentions the author was making. I designated select days for reading and book club discussions and other class periods for writing workshop. On other days the classwork overlapped and reading and discussion happened in social studies and in ELA.

Google Lit Trips

Meanwhile, Francesca had her social studies students track their character's journey from their book club reading book using Google Maps. Google Tour Creator lets you create your own "3-D trip" by adding or pinning stops and landmarks on the map with images from Google Street View or 360 photos. Students visually recorded what happened to their character during the Holocaust. Some were forced to move from their home and homeland, while others went into hiding or were able to escape. What choices did they make, and where did they go? These questions guided the students in mapping out the story. Students had to write short summaries of the events and locations in their book, as well. The assignment was similar to a Google Lit Trip. Google Lit Trips are downloadable files that feature a book's key locations mapped on Google Earth that can be used for following a character's journey virtually and learn additional information related to the text, setting, and events. Students and teachers can use ready-made trips, or for higher-thinking skills, students can create their own interactive Google Lit Trips to upload. Some of the book titles you can find in the Lit Trip Library include *Long Walk to Water* (Sue Monk Kidd), *Bud Not Buddy* (Christopher Paul Curtis), and *Hana's Suitcase* (Karen Levine), a Holocaust book for young readers that investigates the fate of Hana Brady during the Holocaust.

A Multigenre Project

As you've seen, before writing begins, students are immersed reading about many facets of the era. Students are informed and inspired by their book club reading, as well as by read-alouds and close readings in English and social studies class. All of these reading experiences leave lasting impressions on the students about the atrocities and inspiring acts that people experienced during this time. In social studies class, students read and learn about propaganda, anti-Semitism, Hitler, and the rise of Nazism. In English, students read poems, vignettes, and diary entries written by teenagers about these events. All the while, students participate in jigsaws, learning stations, and discussions that immerse them in the facts about the events that led up to World War II and the Holocaust.

After a week of lessons on the events that led up to the Holocaust, we introduce the culminating assignment and pass out the project organizer (**Figure 2.2**) to help students focus their research and inquiry during the remaining weeks of the unit. To begin, students pick their topic. The topics and themes listed in the organizer parallel topics that students have read about in their book club books. Students can write about a theme similar to what they have been reading about or choose a theme or topic that is a question they still want to know more about. The next step in the organizer, formulating a claim about the topic or theme, is almost always a challenge for students. Whether you call it a claim (as based on the New York State ELA exam) or a thesis, which is the more common term in high school and college, the statement is central to the direction of their project. We conducted this unit during the spring so students would already have had a lot of practice writing claims for literary essays and feature articles.

In middle school, students are taught that the claim is the main argument of their writing. A claim defines the paper's goals, direction, and scope and is supported by evidence, quotations, argumentation, expert opinion, statistics, and telling details. Students need practice and opportunities to read, write, and revise claims throughout the writing process. I use the graphic organizer in **Figure 2.3** in writing lessons and activities to help students write their own claims after looking at many models and examples of writing. Make sure students realize their claim is not a one-and-done task; they might need to revise it throughout the writing process in order to craft a claim that is clear, specific, and articulates the "so what" of the piece.

To help students formulate their claims and projects, I model my own writing process under a document camera, projecting my writing on the SMART Board. Students need to see writing in action; don't leave them to write independently and in isolation—where they may struggle to begin or elaborate. Educator and author Penny Kittle explained the benefits of modeling writing, saying, "I write beside them. My process is a bridge for students. I confer with readers and writers daily and teach into their intentions, meeting with them where they are and nudging them forward. Conferences multiply the proximity" (2018, pg. 31). Writing conferences and writing together in the classroom help students practice writing and get immediate feedback from their teacher. When teachers model for students and offer models of good writing, students see the process of articulating thinking on paper. Students can borrow transition moves and structure to help formulate their own thinking—from you as well as from the writers they are reading.

MULTIGENRE PROJECT ORGANIZER
5 SOURCES, CREATIVE PIECES, 5 GENRE

1. Choose one of the Topics/Themes below *(circle your topic choice)*:

Upstanders	Bystanders	Victims	Perpetrators	Resistance
Nationalism	Choices	Universe of Obligation	Collaborators	Rescuers

2. Formulate a Claim/Thesis about the Topic/Theme:

A claim is not one word. It is not a phrase. It *is* a statement that attempts to create an explanation worthy of thought and analysis. Think back to the sophisticated theme topic you developed in your notebook based on your independent reading book. Draft your claim below.

Example Claims:

Resistance to the Nazis was not easy and required deep courage that not all human beings possess.

It was much easier for German citizens and conquered people to become bystanders and shut their eyes to the atrocities of the Nazis.

Nationalism is a powerful force for both good and bad and can lead citizens down a dangerous and scary path.

_____

_____

_____

_____

_____

3. Select Genres/Projects:

Incorporate five different genre pieces, each anchored in a primary source, to convey the depth and complexity of the theme presented in World War II. In the reflection at the end of the project, you will articulate your understanding, knowledge, and purpose in selecting the primary sources and how each has informed your thinking about the topic. Be sure to include the five sources and a Works Cited page with the final project.

FIGURE 2.2 Students use the Multigenre Project Organizer to help brainstorm and plan their final project.

PRIMARY SOURCES (CIRCLE 5 SOURCES)				
Photographs	Direct Quotes	Government Documents	Letters	Diary Entries
Speeches	Propaganda Posters	Political Cartoons	Poetry	Interviews
Maps	Artwork			

GENRES (CIRCLE 5 GENRES YOU WILL WRITE)				
Poem	Historical Fiction	Comic Book Excerpt	Drawing	Narrative
Letter	Diary Entry	Speech	Interview	Monologue
Internal Dialogue	Play	Vignette		

As you research and create, you need to consider your topic and think about which genres would be effective to communicate your ideas/impressions. Before you select each genre for your project, ask yourself, "Why am I choosing this genre? What do I want to be able to say or express through this genre?" If you can't answer those questions, you are not ready to work on it. Your choices must be intentional and have a purpose.

Additional Items

4. Letter to the Reader:

    Your Letter to the Reader is an invitation for your reader. In three paragraphs, you will address the following:

    - Introduce your topic and thesis. How did you come to select this theme? What personal connections have you made?

    - What primary sources and research did you use? How did these primary sources impact the pieces you wrote? Explain the order of the genres you selected.

    - How has your research and writing opened your eyes to World War II? What have you learned and what do you want your readers to take away?

5. Reflection/Coda at the end of the multigenre project:

    Address the following questions:

    - How do choices define us?

    - What are the consequences of not remembering World War II and the Holocaust?

    - How does the past influence your actions and treatment of others after your research and writing about World War II? What have you learned by completing this project?

    - Which multigenre piece you wrote are you most proud of and why?

FIGURE 2.3

A graphic organizer can help students write a claim or thesis.

WRITING A CLAIM IN 3 STEPS

Directions: Insert your original thesis below.

Does it meet all 3 requirements? Revise what is needed to complete all elements of your claim.

MAKE TOPIC SPECIFIC	CONTINUE WITH DESCRIPTIVE OR DEBATABLE PHRASE	EXPLAIN THE SIGNIFICANCE TO YOUR AUDIENCE
Exactly who? When? How many? Which ones? Where?	Does…, Does not…, Should…, Should not…, Ignores…, Highlights…	Providing that…, Resulting in…

Students had ten class periods to complete their multigenre projects and completed the majority of their research and writing during class time. While my students were working on their projects, I also wrote a Letter to the Reader and one genre piece, a survivor's letter to captured Nazi Adolf Eichmann, as a model for them (**Figure 2.4**). In addition to finding primary sources and writing their responses, students also had to introduce each piece to the reader, elaborate on the origin of its primary source, and include background information for the reader. I used my Letter to the Reader to give an overview of the project and explanation of my claim.

As a class we had read the Author's Note in Ruta Sepetys' *Salt of the Sea* and discussed how the author used it to shed additional light on both her fictional characters and the actual events on which her story was based. As a model for their own introductions and author's notes, students used Sepetys' statement, "The child and young adult narrative is **what I chose to represent in the novel**, seeing the war through the eyes of youths from different nations, forced to leave everything they loved behind" (2016, p. 382). As a result, the student's introductions were forthright in showing their research and understanding as well as empathy and compassion. **Figure 2.5**

Morgan's Project

highlights Morgan's introductions and creative writing pieces as an example of what students wrote. (To read Morgan's multigenre project in its entirety, scan the QR code here.)

Throughout the multigenre project, students were "gathering, interpreting, and using evidence" (NY Grade 8 Social Studies Standards) from diverse sources to identify and connect to their claim. Guided by the school databases and websites we teachers provided, students identified works of art, photographs, charts, documentaries, memoirs, and other primary and secondary sources to help curate their project and inform their investigation. Then students analyzed and made inferences to develop and support their claim. Just as the sources came in many forms, students could choose which creative writing forms to connect to the historical documents and articulate their claim. Morgan's piece included historical fiction, poetry, a diary entry, and a letter, for instance. Depending on the students in your classroom, offering artistic responses in addition to creative writing can empower struggling writers. For ELL students, allowing them to create photographs and artistic responses ties content together and shows their understanding. The artwork that many of my students created enhanced the meaning of the explanation and arguments they were making. As a result of student choice and creative freedom, the projects were thoughtful and persuasive.

In the introduction of her multigenre project, Morgan stated, "My research and writing has given me an entirely new perspective on World War II and the Holocaust. It has allowed me to read many pieces of writing by people who experienced the Holocaust and put myself in their shoes." Morgan was not the only student who mentioned the depth of understanding acquired throughout the unit. Dylan wrote in his Coda, "My research and writing has made me understand how many different ways there were of resisting the Holocaust, and how hard it often was not to lose hope. I want my readers to know that every act of resistance matters, and I myself have learned that I can make a difference."

Reading and writing helps expand our worldview and build compassion for others. Some say we learn history so that we do not repeat the past. We read stories so that we can see ourselves and others in books to remind us that we are not alone. If we want students to be leaders and help make the world a better place, empathy and compassion need to be part of the curriculum.

Dear Reader,

Everyday we make choices: what to eat, what to wear, what to say, what to do. We have the freedom to makes choice. Choices and freedom are a luxury. And then there are places and periods in history when freedoms are lost and choices are life and death matters. During World War II and the Holocaust, some people had choices and others did not— they were following orders. Orders to move, orders to kill, orders to die. During this time period more than 11 million people died. 6 million were Jewish. 1.5 million were children. Through stories, movies, images, and photographs we are witness to the atrocities that occurred throughout the world. We are witness to the choices that people made to be upstanders or to be bystanders: to resist or to follow orders. We can never say whether a victim had a choice. It is clear that people had to make very difficult choices during this time. After the war, the choices that followed were just as complex. ***What I chose to represent in this multigenre project*** *are the difficult choices that many people had to make during the war and also after the war.* None of these choices were easy and each bears consequences, risks, rewards, life, and death.

The first primary source is a photograph of Nazi war criminal, Adolf Eichmann. He was one of the high-ranking SS men under Hitler who decided to move the Jews into ghettos. Eichmann also established the Final Solution, the Nazi plan to exterminate all of the Jews in Europe and eventually, the world. After World War II when Germany surrendered, Eichmann was one of the Nazis to escape and change his identity. He lived in Europe for five years after the war under an assumed name and then moved to Argentina where he lived a full life, hiding from his past crimes. An organization of Nazi hunters searched for Eichmann and other war criminals after the war and were informed by a Holocaust survivor of Eichmann's whereabouts.

Photograph of Nazi War Criminal Adolf Eichmann on trial in Jerusalem, 1961.

Retrieved from www.jewishvirtuallibrary.org/ the-capture-of-nazi-criminal-adolf-eichmann

LETTER FROM A HOLOCAUST SURVIVOR TO ADOLF EICHMANN

1961

Dear Adolf Eichmann,

I have lost my entire family. My mama, my papa, my brothers, and sisters. Their spouses and even my four-month-old niece who will never be able to grow up. We were stuffed into cattle cars to places that were only rumored about. The lack of air, the lack of space, privacy. The horrors people talked about as we were taken away. This was all part of your plan. The Final Solution you formulated to make Germany great again. After four days and three nights traveling to Auschwitz we were able to sense the danger ahead. As soon as the car doors opened, the gray sky was looming above and the air was thick with ashes clouding the sky like snowflakes. The dogs were barking and soldiers with their guns pointed us in different directions. Some to our deaths and others selected to work to death.

My family tree is missing many branches because of your plan and yet, you announce to the world, after your capture that you were only acting "under orders" and that you were just "a cog in the machine" doing what you had been told. You take no accountability. You show no remorse as I and those who survive weep for our families we will never see again. 11 million missing branches.

And yet, I am starting new again. I watch your trial in my living room in my new home in America with my wife and children who I say nothing to about my past. I do not want to live in the past. I am choosing to live for the future and help my family tree flourish and grow despite the branches that were destroyed by you and the Nazis. As I listen to you stand on trial, I see and hear no remorse from you. You are matter of fact. But let's be clear—you made a choice. A choice to follow and a choice to obey. I am making a choice now and moving forward. My choice is not to hate, despite the hate that I experienced in my youth. My choice is to love unconditionally and live everyday for my family and for all the people who are no longer here. We make choices daily. My choice is to live.

Sincerely,

Abe Moskowitz

FIGURE 2.4 To acquaint students with the elements of the multigenre project, I created this sample Letter to the Reader, cited one primary source, and wrote a creative response.

Dear Reader,

What do you think of when you hear the word "strength?" Some people think of physical strength, while others think of inner strength. Throughout my multigenre project, it is up to you to interpret which type the Holocaust victims needed to endure that barbaric time. During the Holocaust, people were abruptly taken from their homes and transported to concentration camps to either die or be worked to death. They faced every obstacle imaginable and learned along the way what strength really means. Food, water, and rest are the three things that keep us alive. At the concentration camps and ghettos, these three elements of life were luxuries. While working your fingers bloody so you can receive a food ration the Nazis would scream that you are pigs. You have no worth and don't even count as a human being. You would always live in constant fear of them killing you. Killing you for no other reason than they see you as a burden on society for doing nothing. By simply being yourself and who you were born to be you are told that this is not enough. That they want to exterminate you and many alike solely because of something you cannot change. Holocaust victims had to be strong, not letting the hate they received affect them and the atrocious events they experienced lower their hope or determination. What I choose to represent in this multigenre project is that Holocaust victims possessed a deep kind of strength that allowed them to persevere in the face of death. Through my research on World War II and the Holocaust, I have learned that sometimes it is the quiet strength that roars in the midst of chaos.

My research and writing has given me an entirely new perspective on World War 2 and the Holocaust. It has allowed me to read many pieces of writing by people who experienced the Holocaust and put myself in their shoes. Holocaust victims were told their life is worthless but they didn't give up. Everything was taken from them. The Nazis stole lives, and people cannot be replaced. Yet they persevere., because no matter how much they have lost, they will not let the Nazis win. Some even risk their lives by documenting the Holocaust so people will know forever what happened when Hitler took over. Holocaust survivors are not defined by their strength, it is their decision to be strong that allowed them to endure pain, the injustice, and ultimately win the battle.

I.

This Historical Fiction piece is from the perspective of 16 year old Nadette, and her struggle to take care of her two younger sisters in a concentration camp. They are Jewish and have not yet been killed, but live in constant fear of it. I include a quote from Hitler because it has information relevant to Nadette. Although this is not good news, it only wills Nadette further to make sure her sisters survive even if it means she doesn't.

"Wake up, Nadette," my youngest sister, Alvina, whispered sweetly. For a moment I was home, I was lying in my warm bed hugged by my silky sheets. I could hear my little sisters giggling and my father's warm laugh downstairs. Mother was humming from outside my window as she watered the flowers. The sugary smell of french toast wafted into my lilac room. "Quickly, Nadette," the anxious sound of Etha's voice willed me to get up. Although Etha was only 2 years older than 8 year old Alvina, she has already lost the joyous outlook on life. My back ached from the cold, hard ground we slept on. My sisters and I rushed to get ready, layering every item of clothing we brought with us to fight against the cold. Our small hut was about six feet by six feet and just barely squeezed us inside. We were thrown inside it when we arrived here, its previous owners no longer here. The hut was stuck together by a few pieces of wood with dirt in between. Seventy-two tally marks were scratched on the hut just above the bark we used as a door. Every night I fall asleep wondering what happened to whoever scratched those markings.

"We need to go NOW," Etha commanded. We ducked out the door and speedily walked to the center of the camp for roll call. At exactly four every morning we all file in for role call. Yesterday a young boy and his mother were beaten for arriving late, it was heartbreaking.

Role call lasts hours, some of the injured or sick even die during it. Snow, rain, hail, no matter the weather we go to roll call. But we cannot complain and must look healthy or else we are taken away. I don't allow my mind to wonder where they take people. My heart is finally getting used to constantly racing, but my mind will never. Sometimes when the Nazis aren't looking I risk holding my sisters hands, we all need the strength. I spend most of roll call with my eyes closed, picturing myself at home. I let my mind wander to my old cream colored house surrounded by the yellow tulips that grow every year. And the smell of earth and summer that never seemed to leave our home. Etha secretly steps on my toes, pulling me from my daydream when the guards were about to look our way.

Role call finally ends and we are sent off to do work. My sisters went off to fish, but the fish is only for the Nazis, we eat watery soup and bread for our meals. I went to work at a factory, producing things for the war. Although we hated our jobs, we were grateful to not do the labor that the men were assigned: hauling boulders up steps. It was pointless. Much of the work that is forced is pointless, but to the Nazis it was amusing to see us suffer.

The day ended and my hands throbbed from the work. I walked by one of the Nazi's houses and slowed as I heard the radio on. Hitler was speaking on a radio broadcast, "We shall only talk of peace when we have won the war. The Jewish capitalist world will not survive the twentieth century." Fear. Fear is eating away at everyone here and I must not let it get to me. My sisters and I are Jews and based on some of the things I have heard from others, it's a miracle we are alive. Even if I don't survive I need to keep Alvina and Etha alive. I must keep them alive. I pushed these worries out of my head as I waited in line to get my food ration and returned to our hut. I ducked inside to see Etha crying on the floor, with Alvina softly comforting her. "What's wrong?" The urgency in my voice was almost tangible. Etha tried to explain through muffled sobs, but Alvina placed a hand on her shoulder, silencing her. "The Nazis said we did not catch enough fish, so they took away or food rations today and tomorrow," Alvina said flatly. My heart sank. How could they do this to children. I gave them my cold bread, "Everything will be okay, think of something happy." I sat there, hugging them until their breathing became slower as they drifted off to sleep. It has to get better. Surely other countries will see what the Nazis are doing and help. Won't they?

FIGURE 2.5 Morgan's introduction and first creative writing pieces for her multigenre project were based on one of Hitler's radio broadcasts during his reign in Nazi Germany.

Digital Possibilities

The writing your students create in their multigenre projects can be powerful and inspiring—so much so that you may want to share their projects with a larger audience. With the help of digital age tools, you can. Using a classroom blog or having students post their own blogs through Kidblog or Google's Blogger enables student writers to reach a wider audience. Whereas blogs allow students to post a written report, such tools as Adobe Spark Video, VoiceThread, and Book Creator enable students to be creative communicators and digital innovators of multimedia text. In today's digital age, it is not only about helping students develop writing skills; they should also be able to build a repertoire of digital writing tools that can "increase learning and communication" (New York State Next Generation Learning Standards, 2017) about the world today, tomorrow, and in the past.

Video Storytelling with Adobe Spark

Free for educators, Adobe Spark for Education is an iOS app that offers templates and lesson plans for creating beautiful visual stories and presentations. This video storytelling application combines motion graphics, audio recording, music, text, and photos and can be used to produce short, narrated, animated videos. Students and teachers can choose their own design or pick from a number of templates based on the structure of the story to be told and then add photos, text, and audio narration to make a digital creation. Colette Cassinelli, a library instructional technology teacher at Sunset High School in Oregon's Beaverton School District, used Adobe Spark Video to help her school's English teachers extend a narrative unit on reading memoirs. Students wrote their own personal narratives, then recorded them using Adobe Spark.

Voice Poems with VoiceThread

Similar to Adobe Spark, VoiceThread is a platform where students can collaborate and present visual and print text, as well as add comments on each other's work through video, audio, and text. With the help of her school's instructional technology specialist, teacher Lynette Hull created an inspiring VoiceThread project with her fifth-grade students at the Wekiva Elementary School in Longwood, Florida. To help her students understand the challenges that people endured living through the Great Depression, Hull had pairs of students select one of Dorothea Lange's moving Depression-era photographs and write two voice poems from the perspectives of the individuals in the photographs. The poems were then recorded and posted on VoiceThread with the images from Lange. The voice poem pairs are written from two different points of view about the same topic, so the students sometimes speak in dialogue and others in unison. You can scan the QR code or visit goo.gl/E8BdPk to experience this project, which includes three mediums: visual, print, and audio. Viewers can listen and view the creative writing pieces and then leave audio or written feedback on the student's projects.

Voice
Poem Example

Hull's project had many elements to enhance students' understanding of this time period and build empathy for others. Students first had to be critical observers of images, then researchers about the Great Depression, and finally creative writers and communicators while working with a partner. Teaching writing today is about introducing different mediums to students and allowing them to choose the best medium for their message or story.

Book Creator

Available for iOS and in Google Chrome, Book Creator also lets you combine text, audio, video, and visuals to create interactive stories, books, comic adventures, and reports. Students can use this platform for reading and writing. With Book Creator, teachers and students can record their voice, use text to speech to dictate their writing, translate their book into different languages, search a library of free-use images to add to any book, use the comic template to create storyboards and comics, and also use hyperlinks to create a choose-your-route story. I have seen teachers use book creators

for traditional classroom assessments, such as a book report or reading journal, but with the platform, students can be creative communicators and decision makers about their writing topics and break out of the limited school-assigned genres. Book Creator offers teachers one library with forty books for free; additional costs depend on the number of libraries and books created.

Key Points

A multigenre project can be adapted for any subject and scaled to any size. If five creative responses are too many for your students to write, have them create two or three instead. Whereas my eighth graders were studying World War II and the Holocaust, seventh graders could explain the impact of government policies on early United States and Colonial North America. Fifth graders could write multigenre projects based on communities in the Western Hemisphere or people's experiences during Westward Expansion. Students could collaborate with writing partners or as a whole class to create a multigenre project on immigration. If students are having trouble finding primary sources, you might provide text and images for students to respond to. For instance, try a Photograph Flood activity: I spread one hundred laminated images across the desks or around the classroom for students to look through and choose one or two that stand out to them. Students then go back to their desks to write down what they see in the picture and brainstorm questions they have about the picture.

Choice motivates students. Multigenre projects allow students to purposefully choose the best genres to showcase their research, learning, and understanding. Each piece might work independently to make a point, but together they create a symphony of perspectives and depth on a subject, theme, or topic. The project can have many voices and multiple authors. As knowledge constructors in this unit, students create "writing collections to demonstrate the interconnectedness" (New York State Next Generation Writing Standards, 2017) of the human experience and are creative communicators publishing their writing for a greater audience to inform their interpretations of history.

Moving forward, I return to a traditional secondary writing assignment: the essay. In an age of expanding digital instructional tools and writing formats, how can teachers use technology to support writing this traditional assessment while at the same time honoring student voice and agency? Chapter Three offers some suggestions.

TABLE 2.1 Tools, Strategies, and Standards

Teaching Techniques & Strategies	Resources	Links	ISTE Standards for Educators and for Students	Common Core State Standards
Resources for Teaching World War II and the Holocaust	Facing History	facinghistory.org	(E) 1. Learner Educators continually improve their practice by learning from and with others and exploring proven and promising practices that leverage technology to improve student learning.	CCSS.ELA-Literacy.RH.6-8.10 By the end of grade 8, read and comprehend history/social studies texts in the grades 6-8 text complexity band independently and proficiently.
Virtual Story Mapping	Google Lit Trips Google Tour Creator	googlelittrips.org vr.google.com/tourcreator	(S) 3d. Knowledge Constructor Students build knowledge by actively exploring real-world issues and problems, developing ideas and theories and pursuing answers and solutions.	CCSS.ELA-Literacy.RL.8.2 Determine a theme or central idea of a text and analyze its development over the course of the text, including its relationship to the characters, setting, and plot; provide an objective summary of the text.
Digital Publishing	Adobe Spark Video Blogger Book Creator Kidblog VoiceThread	spark.adobe.com/edu blogger.com bookcreator.com kidblog.org voicethread.com/products/k12	(S) 3c. Knowledge Constructor Students curate information from digital resources using a variety of tools and methods to create collections of artifacts that demonstrate meaningful connections or conclusions. (S) 6d. Creative Communicator Students publish or present content that customizes the message and medium for their intended audiences.	CCSS.ELA-Literacy.W.8.3 Write narratives to develop real or imagined experiences or events using effective technique, relevant descriptive details, and well-structured event sequences. CCSS.ELA-Literacy.W.8.6 Use technology, including the Internet, to produce and publish writing and present the relationships between information and ideas efficiently as well as to interact and collaborate with others.

Essay Writing

Essay writing is the foundation of secondary school. As much as I desire to focus exclusively on creative writing and diverse formats in my classroom, that is not the reality. Students work on literary essays throughout their schooling, learning and writing in a format that exists across content subjects, standardized tests, and throughout college. Students learn the five-paragraph essay format in order to articulate their thinking about their reading and showcase their understanding. How do we help students to do that, while at the same time show original thinking about their reading, include textual evidence, as well as maintain voice and individuality? We work on it word by word, sentence by sentence, and paragraph by paragraph, through models and mentor texts, discussions, and scaffolds. I think of Anne Lamott and her description in her book *Bird By Bird* (1995):

> *Thirty years ago my older brother, who was ten years old at the time, was trying to get a report on birds written that he'd had three months to write. It was due the next day. We were out at our family cabin in Bolinas, and he was at the kitchen table close to tears, surrounded by binder paper and pencils and unopened books on birds, immobilized by the hugeness of the task ahead. Then my father sat down beside him, put his arm around my brother's shoulder, and said, "Bird by bird, buddy. Just take it bird by bird." (p. 19)*

In this chapter, I will address strategies for teaching essay writing while also bolstering student voice and choice and developing budding writers. Throughout this chapter I share activities and aids I have developed to teach writing, scaffold writing workshops, and support all writers in my classroom. There is no one way to teach writing, and so I also borrow and adapt from current research to better reach the needs of my students and help them meet writing standards to be effective and critical communicators. The chapter also touches on technology options to help students when writing and revising their essays.

Start with Sentence Work

Creator of the Hochman Method and co-author of *The Writing Revolution* (2017), Dr. Judith C. Hochman advises starting small with sentences to help students string words together with poetry, grace, and meaning. Focusing on sentences improves the substance of writing to raise the level of linguistic complexity and clarity, enhance revision and editing skills, and improve reading comprehension. Hochman recommends eight sentence activities to help raise the level of writing among students. These activities can be completed as a warm-up exercise or hook at the beginning of the class, a formative assessment at the end of a lesson, or can be used for station work to help students build a strong foundation for their writing (Hochman, 2018). The two sentence activities that I use the most for students to practice and develop their writing are *sentence fragments* and *Because, But, So.*

Sentence fragments are groups of words that are not a grammatically complete sentence. Usually a fragment lacks a subject, verb, or both or is a dependent clause that is not attached to an independent clause. Teachers can post sentence fragments for students to repair, build on, or revise to add what's missing. The aim of this writing exercise is to grammatically address what is necessary to write complete sentences. For a bell ringer exercise, for example, you might have students identify sentence fragments and change them into complete sentences by adding necessary words, capitalization, and punctuation. **Figure 3.1** showcases an example of the sentence fragments students turned into sentences after reading and acting out Act I, Scene i of Shakespeare's *A Midsummer Night's Dream*. This exercise not only addressed writing and grammar activity, but served as a reading comprehension check for understanding. From student responses, I was able to assess their understanding of the text while they practiced writing complete sentences that were grammatically correct. To reinforce grammar and usage the next day, I shared the sentences that stood out as exemplars. We discussed the elements that made each example sentence clear, articulate, and strong.

Another Hochman sentence building activity that I use often with my students to expand their writing skill utilizes the conjunctions *because, but,* and *so.* Students extend simple sentences with these three conjunctions to

Sentence Fragments	Complete Sentences
Directions – *From the sentence fragments below, create a complete sentence for each fragment based on the play.* 1. Theseus' palace 2. Hippolyta 3. Egeus is angry 4. Hermia's choices 5. the course of true love 6. plan for escape	Hermia and Lysander talk in Theseus' Palace about their plan for escape. Hippolyta is being forced to marry Theseus, but is surprisingly happy. Hermia's choices show that she will do anything for love. Egeus is angry because his daughter is not listening to him. Lysander states, "The course of true love never runs smooth."

FIGURE 3.1 You can use a sentence fragment activity to practice writing or as a formative assessment to check for understanding. After reading *A Midsummer Night's Dream*, students converted fragments (left) into strong sentences (right) that reflected their knowledge of the play.

help learn linguistically complex language that can assist them in writing counterclaims—a useful skill when writing analytical, literary essays. The activity gives students practice extending a sentence into a new direction using one of these conjunctions: *because* to tell why, *but* to introduce a counter-thought, and *so* to show cause and effect. If we want students to think critically and not regurgitate information, we can have students practice, and be sure to give them practice with additional transition words and phrases too, such as *although*, *while*, *even though*, *however*, and *on the other hand*. **Figure 3.2** shows a Because, But, So activity my students completed during the World War II multigenre unit described in Chapter 2.

FIGURE 3.2
Students complete the simple sentence starters using *because*, *but*, and *so* to add complexity and expand their thinking.

Because, But, So

The legal and humanitarian frameworks designating the rights of refugees were established in the wake of World War II because

_____ .

The legal and humanitarian frameworks designating the rights of refugees were established in the wake of World War II, but

_____ .

The legal and humanitarian frameworks designating the rights of refugees were established in the wake of World War II, so

_____ .

INTERACTIVE RESOURCE NOTEBOOKS

Interactive notebooks are tools for teachers and students to engage, organize, and encourage critical thinking. Although the three- and two-dimensional interactive graphic organizers in my students' notebooks are targeted to ELA topics, you can create similar tools to be used at any level and with any subject area as a learning and assessment tool, as well as a portfolio of learning and student-created textbook.

For example, in *Personalized Reading: Digital Tools and Strategies to Support All Learners* (2018), I described how I flip writing lessons, providing videos and notebook resources to help students develop their essays. I create videos and screencasts, then embed them on Google Classroom for students to access at any point during the school year. To coincide with these videos, I create graphic organizers and fold-ables that students insert into their notebook

as reference tools to apply to their reading and writing (**Figure 3.3**). Each student's notebook contains strategies for starting their essays and an ever-growing collection of interactive fold-ables for writing an introduction, building better body paragraphs, writing conclusions, and more. Rather than a static note repository, an interactive notebook is an important tool that students constantly build throughout the school year. It is a tool for students to return to often for writing, review, and reflection.

We know that in the real world, scientists, writers, mathematicians, and historians all keep notebooks to collect their ideas, hypotheses, artifacts, and notes related to their interests and studies. It seems a natural fit for students to do the same in the classroom to compile theories about reading and generating writing ideas.

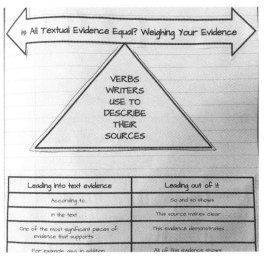
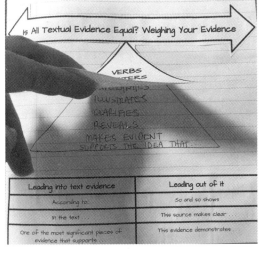

FIGURE 3.3 Two examples of interactive notebook resources: I created a table with sentence starters leading into and out of textual evidence (left) and a word bank with verbs to describe evidence (right) in writing.

Students can complete their sentence activities in their writer's notebooks, on a large note card that you collect at the end of the period, or in digital form. For example, you could compile all student work on a Google Slides deck. To do so, first share a Google Slides deck with the class and then have each student add a new slide with their completed sentences written. I do not grade these sentence activities but use them as a check for understanding and mini-grammar lessons with my student writers.

Building Better Paragraphs

From middle school to high school in my district, we teach a structure for essays, a writing recipe that can help developing student writers in secondary schooling. At the same time, for my stronger writers I offer mini-lessons with writing options and rhetorical moves writers make that highlight their voice and agency in their essays. All students first learn the recipe, and then they are able to adapt and develop throughout their schooling. The writing recipe is simple to remember and effective for students who need a bit more support. For the introductory paragraphs, students follow the ABC approach, and then use TEXAS to help support their claims when writing body paragraphs. Both the ABC and TEXAS strategies help guide students and showcase their thinking.

Structure

Let's break down an ABC introductory paragraph first. The A stands for *attention-grabbing hook*, which is the first line of the essay. It has to hook readers and draw them into the essay. The B stands for *background* information, and in this middle part of the introductory paragraph, students need to include any necessary background information and context that readers need to know as they continue reading. Finally, C is the *claim* (or thesis). Although the last line of the introductory paragraph, the claim is the heart of the essay that marks the argument of the paper. I teach mini-lessons on different strategies to start an essay, and we spend lots of time writing and revising claims to match the intention of the essay.

When writing essay body paragraphs, students follow the acronym TEXAS:

❖ **T**opic sentence

❖ Cont**E**xt

❖ Textual e**X**ample

❖ **A**nalysis

❖ **S**o what?

This format helps students include textual evidence and analysis of how the evidence supports the claim.

Body paragraphs are the meat of an essay. Body paragraphs contain some background information to build context for the reader, but the paragraphs' primary role is to provide evidence that helps support the writer's claim. Listing textual evidence does not make a successful body paragraph; the writer needs to show the connections between the evidence and thesis for the reader. I remind students that when writing we have to connect the dots for readers to help them see the picture of our thinking exposed on the page.

Evidence

Without evidence a body paragraph is doomed to fail, so take time to work with students on collecting evidence that best supports their claims. For example, author and educator Luke Reynolds has his students gather six quotes that they can use to *prove their thesis*. Students explore the text they are reading, find six supporting quotes, and record them on a graphic organizer. After each quote, students must include the quote's page number in parentheses to properly cite the text.

Using a digital mind-mapping or graphics tool can help students catalog and curate the best textual evidence to support their claims, as well. Two good (and free) choices are Popplet and MindMeister. With Popplet, students can brainstorm preliminary writing ideas or curate their textual evidence by pasting boxes (called Popples) that contain text, videos, images, comments, or clip art onto a board. Popples can even contain links to one another, enabling students to connect the dots of their evidence. Similarly, students can

use MindMeister to create diagrams and mind maps to connect thoughts and ideas for writing. Both of these digital tools are collaborative so students can work together to mine a text for evidence.

Analysis

Once students gather their evidence, they must then provide analysis of that textual evidence, describing how it supports their claim. Whether identifying a theme or literary criticism, this is the hardest part for my middle-school students. Many will plop a textual quote into the paragraph and then state, "This quote proves…" Most often, the information doesn't prove anything. To help them, I provide a mini-lesson on how to include textual evidence to showcase their thinking in their writing. Students need scaffolds and academic language to help lead in and out of textual evidence. To see the flipped video I created about leading into and out of textual evidence and getting started with textual analysis, scan the QR code or go to youtu.be/bFAGy5DEuTA.

Textual
Evidence Video

Good analysis is a detailed examination of evidence. But how do students know what to say in the analysis? I tell my students to get rid of the word *proves* and begin with the phrase "*This shows that*" instead to encourage students to articulate why their quote is appropriate. This forces students to explain and elaborate on their thinking without summarizing. Reminding students to put to use the skills they practiced in the Because, But, So exercise can help too, because it forces students to expand their thinking and articulate their reasoning. The graphic organizer in **Figure 3.4** helps simplify and guide students through this body paragraph process.

Particularly for my ELL students who might not have the words or academic language just yet, providing these graphic organizers and sentence stems can help students develop the writing muscles and vocabulary necessary for academic writing. Depending on the writing task, you can adapt your graphic organizers and sentence stems to fit the prompt. For example, suppose you have a short response assignment that requires students to identify a character trait of a book's protagonist and use two direct examples (textual quotes) from their reading to support their answer. In this case, I give my students

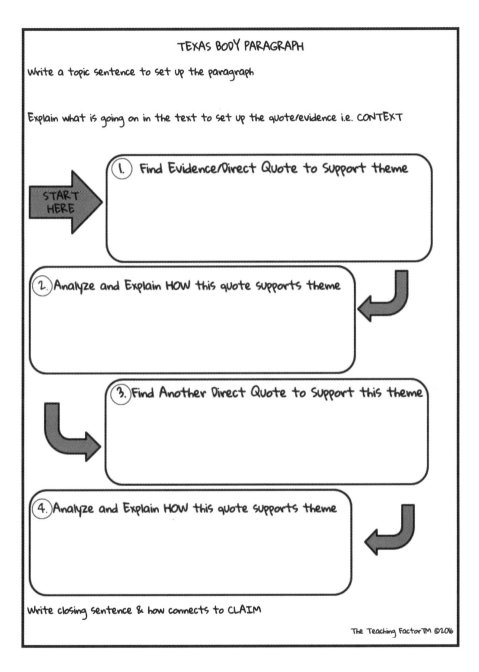

TEXAS BODY PARAGRAPH

Write a topic sentence to set up the paragraph

Explain what is going on in the text to set up the quote/evidence i.e. CONTEXT

START HERE

1. Find Evidence/Direct Quote to support theme

2. Analyze and Explain HOW this quote supports theme

3. Find Another Direct Quote to support this theme

4. Analyze and Explain HOW this quote supports theme

Write closing sentence & how connects to CLAIM

The Teaching Factor™ ©2016

FIGURE 3.4
Providing graphic organizers helps to scaffold student thinking and build academic vocabulary.

four character traits, ask them to choose the one that best fits their protagonist, and have them write a short response to support their choice. To help my ELL and students who need extra support, I also provide the organizer shown in **Figure 3.5** to break down the task into manageable parts and help students articulate their understanding.

Characterization refers both to the personality of a character and the way in which an author reveals that personality. A character's personality is made up of different qualities, or character traits, that the reader discovers as the work unfolds. An author often gives characters several different traits to make them seem real and believable.

1. Circle the word that best identifies the character trait of the main character in your book:

   Mental Strength   **Optimistic**   **Integrity**   **Intelligence**

2. Why does this character trait work for the main character in your book?

3. What is the definition of the character trait you selected?

Character Trait	Definition

4. Complete the table below:

What Textual Evidence supports this Character Trait	How does this quote SHOW the Character Trait *How does this demonstrate the trait?*
Page #	
Page #	

5. Putting Our Ideas Together in a Short Response - Use these sentence stems to help you write your short response.

   In the book _____, the protagonist _____ demonstrates the character trait _____. To have _____ means to _____. This is illustrated when _____ says, _____. This shows _____ because _____. Additionally, when _____ says, _____ s/he is demonstrating _____ because _____. Having _____ (insert character trait) helps to _____.

FIGURE 3.5 This scaffolding exercise provides additional support for students who struggle with writing and developing academic language.

Digital Supports

I am always developing writing activities and supports for the diverse students in my classroom, but you may prefer a digital approach. Integrated with G Suite, Google Classroom, and Schoology, Writable is a guided writing practice program for grades 3–12 that helps you and your students (**Figure 3.6**). For students, the platform models writing by demonstrating key skills, strategies, and techniques to use. Writable offers checklists and comment stems to help students write, revise, and reflect on their writing. Writable enables you to extend writing practice from instruction: You can select Writable's assignments, rubrics, and prompts, or import your own. To preview or customize any of the assignments on the Writable platform, you can sign up for a free sixty-day trial, but to use Writable long term you must subscribe.

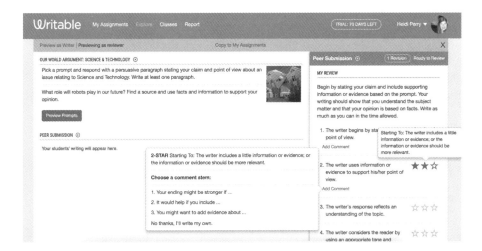

FIGURE 3.6
The Writable writing platform offers exercises and supports for student writing.

With more than 600 prompts, Writable offers plenty of opportunities for practicing writing for short responses, essays, and quick writes. The platform contains assignments from Smarter Balanced Assessment and can be used for standardized test preparation or academic intervention. For students who are in literacy classes for extended support, for example, a digital platform like Writable offers the teacher and students the necessary guided supports and material to help increase writing skills and practice.

Revision Opportunities

Writing is a lifelong skill, and the more students write, the better they develop as writers and communicators. This requires that students write daily and have opportunities to revise their writing. With revision opportunities, students are able to reexamine their writing with a critical eye and grow as writers. Give students time to peer edit their writing, talk to one another about their writing, and swap Chromebooks to read each other's work. During writing conferences, ask students how you can help them. Sometimes I collect and read through first drafts to give students feedback so they can revise their work to meet the benchmarks and learning targets. I also save student essays to use as exemplars or models for my students during mini-lessons in following years. My essay prompts are always changing and evolving, but I use these student models to showcase writing that was done exceptionally well.

Revision is an important part of the writing process and can be utilized in ways that empower student writers. For instance, I use revision passports, revision stations, and even adapt revision into a game to allow students to make their writing stronger.

Revision Olympics

After the first literary essay assignment of the school year, my students participate in a revision activity that involves station work and an opportunity to personalize and choose the revision they need to improve their essay. Called the Revision Olympics, the activity consists of five challenges or stations for students to complete in order to come back to their writing with new insight and purpose. Here's a quick tour of the stations:

STATION ONE: STUDENT EXEMPLARS AND REFLECTION. Beginning with a student model, students read through an exemplar and then answer the following reflection questions: What does the student writer do well? What do you want to model or borrow from his or her essay? What is one thing you are going to do differently as a result of reading this student's essay?

STATION TWO: BUILDING BETTER INTRODUCTORY PARAGRAPHS. This station requires students to go back to their draft and read through their introduction. Students pick a checklist to use against their introductory paragraph (**Figure 3.7**). Whether students answer yes or no on the checklist determines if they stay and work more on their introductory paragraph at this station or move on to the next revision station for a grammar check.

Introduction
Checklist

INTRODUCTION CHECKLIST

Directions - Read through your first paragraph and complete the following checklist:

Does your introduction . . .

	YES	NOT YET
Begin with an engaging attention-grabbing statement to hook the reader?		
(Following up on previous question) If yes, how so? Use the space to explain how it engages and captures attention.		
Build background knowledge for the reader without summarizing the entire text?		
Include the text title and author?		
End with a clear claim that states what you are writing about in one clear-cut sentence?		

If you answered "Yes," move on to Station 3.

If you answered "No" to any of the above questions, let's spend some time to revise and make your introduction better. Turn over this checklist to learn how . . .

Front

First impressions are so important. How many times have you heard that? It is true that the first impression—whether it's a first meeting with a person or the first sentence of a paper—sets the stage for a lasting opinion.

In a well-constructed first paragraph, that first sentence will lead into three or four sentences that provide details about the subject or your process you will address in the body of your essay. These sentences should also set the stage for your thesis statement.

The thesis statement is the subject of much instruction and training. The entirety of your paper hangs on that sentence, which is the last sentence of your introductory paragraph.

In summary, your introductory paragraph should contain the following:

- an attention-grabbing first sentence
- informative sentences that build to your thesis
- the thesis statement, which makes a claim or states a view that you will support or build upon

Let's look at a sample intro paragraph and make the necessary edits and revisions on the student example below.

Throughout To Kill a Mockingbird by Harper Lee, the author shows how the title of the book symbolizes a big theme and many characters. She explains to the reader that "it is a sin to kill a mockingbird" and that numerous characters in the book exemplify this.

What does the writer need to do to make it better?

Back

FIGURE 3.7 This station activity has students examine the introduction of their essay by editing another student's writing to construct a better opening paragraph.

Supporting
Evidence Organizer

FIGURE 3.8
Students used
the Finding and
Supporting
Evidence graphic
organizer to
categorize and
weigh the strength
of their evidence to
help support their
essay writing.

STATION THREE: TEXTUAL EVIDENCE AND SUPPORTING YOUR CLAIM. At this station, students are provided with a graphic organizer to review their evidence and analysis. Students are provided with highlighters to code the evidence in their essay and then complete the graphic organizer to share with a writing partner. Working with a writing partner requires students to communicate in writing and speaking to articulate their evidence and how it supports their claims. The writing partner acts as a compass to help the student check that their thinking is clear. **Figure 3.8** below shows the graphic organizer students worked on at Station Three. For a copy to use with your students, scan the QR code (tinyurl.com/y5zxavhg).

Welcome! You and your writing partner are investigators who must determine whether the evidence you have provided in your essay supports your claims.

1. Highlight all the evidence you provide in your essay and complete the first column of the graphic organizer by listing all your evidence. Evidence includes direct textual quotes and paraphrased examples.

2. Next, explain how each piece of evidence supports your claim. If your partner disagrees with your explanation, you must find evidence that will convince them.

3. In the last column, write down what you think the author is trying to prove with this example and why it matters.

STATION FOUR: GRAMMAR CHECK. At their last station, students check grammar, usage, spelling, and mechanics. With Chromebooks in my classroom, I am able to have students access one of many online grammar tools to help them edit their writing. For instance, Ginger for Schools is a free grammar and spelling checker that includes a sentence rephraser, dictionary, spell checker, and text-to-speech reader. Ginger can help students by offering suggestions for different ways to phrase sentences to improve their writing. Similarly, Grammarly EDU offers writing assistance and a plagiarism checker for a fee. Grammarly integrates with Microsoft Office and Chrome. A third online editing tool for writers, ProWritingAid integrates with Microsoft Word and Google Docs and provides students with a summary report about the strengths and weakness of their writing. ProWritingAid monitors the number of times certain words are used and detects passive voice in addition to checking spelling, grammar, and punctuation.

Creating an editing checklist to self-edit or peer edit can help students edit their writing for spelling, punctuation, and grammar, as well as help students to build an awareness of grammatical conventions. (Scan the Editing Checklist QR code for an example from ReadWriteThink.) In addition, encourage students to read their writing aloud as a way to catch such writing pitfalls as run-on sentences, alternating tenses, and unclear or incomplete sentences.

Editing Checklist

Gameboards and HyperDocs

One of the benefits of being a connected educator is that teachers share and inspire one another. Being on Twitter has changed my teaching for the better and has allowed me to connect and collaborate with some of the most amazing educators. One of those educators, Lisa Guardino, shared on Twitter three HyperDoc game boards that she created for students to follow as a revising tool for argument, informative, and narrative writing. (To view the boards, scan the QR code.) Each board offers twelve squares with links to tutorials, activities, checklists, and rubrics for her students to complete and help improve their writing. Inspired by her game boards, I made one

HyperDoc
Gameboard

STAY CONNECTED, KEEP LEARNING

The ISTE Standards for Educators post Learner as the number one standard: "Educators continually improve their practice by learning from and with others and exploring proven and promising practices that leverage technology to improve student learning" (2017). Twitter enables teachers to meet this standard, because it is a tool that allows educators to develop a professional learning network that allows you to learn, share, collaborate, and elevate your teaching. Specifically, you can follow several Twitter chats and hashtags to collaborating and learn more about teaching writing. These include #tcrwp, #2ndaryELA, #teachwrite, and #engchat. Don't just stop at Twitter, you can also follow your favorite writers and teachers of writing and read blogs on teaching writing, such as *Two Writing Teachers*, *Raising Readers and Writers*, and *Trail of Breadcrumbs*. Great teachers are always learning. For the sake of your students, connect, collaborate, and never stop learning.

for my students to use when revising an investigative journalism article (see Chapter One). Similar to Snakes and Ladders, the game allows students to move up and down the board to help revise and edit their writing (**Figure 3.9**). I posted the game board on Google Classroom during a writing workshop, so students could work and revise at their own pace and use the board throughout the writing process.

Invetigative Journalism Snakes & Ladders THIS GAME BOARD IS A GUIDE to writing your investigative journal article. Use each box for step-by-step inspiration to writing and revising your piece.	**FINISH & TURN IT IN!**	**11. Hearing Is Believing** Reading a piece aloud has many benefits. Most have more experience listening and speaking than reading and revising. Aloud = new information. Try recording! Vocaroo	**10. Time for Triage!** *Use the Language Tool* to get some initial grammar and style feedback - quick fixes. Here is the LINK
7. Strong Verbs! While there are many parts of speech in the English language, **the verb works harder and is more important than any other** - it gets things done. Spend some time revising verbs in your argument! VERB LIST	**8. Incubate...** Wait awhile after you've finished a draft before looking at it again. A few hours - a few days. When you return, be honest (not lazy!). What do you truly think about the paper?	**REVISION TIME** *I have rewritten - often several times - every word I have ever written. My pencils outlast their erasers.* - Vladimir Nabovkov	**9. Check** RUBRICS can help us know to how our performance ranks in each criteria and what some possible next steps are. *Take another look at the rubric and your argument.*
6. Find the Perfect Words! Diction refers to the author's choice of words. Words are the basic tools of the writer - just like a painter uses color and a musician uses sound. In order to write well, you have to find the perfect words! Pull out the Thesaurus to raise the level of vocabulary in your article.	**Phone a Friend** Take this moment to share what you have written with a friend in the class or to conference with your teacher. What is working and where do you need to elaborate more?	**5. Why Rhetoric Matters** **Words are powerful tools**. They support ideas, stir passion and anger, and fuel action. Fuel your journalism piece with **ETHOS & PATHOS** - add a personal story or testimony to help convey your message.	**4. Evidence Does Not Speak for Itself!** After evidence is introduced into your argument, you must add how and why it supports the argument. This is based on your annotations & is built in your body paragraphs.
START ➡	**1. The Lede - Hook'em Like a Fish!** How are you going to hook your reader? Use one of the five lede strategies to help draw your reader in, inform them of the topic, and make them want to read more.	**2. What's the Point?** *Does Your Claim Make The Grade?* You might need to elaborate on your lede some more in the beginning before you get to your CLAIM. What is your claim? A solid claim makes an argument - develops an interesting perspective that can be supported & defended. It must be more than just a simple observation. It will inspire multiple perspectives.	**3. Zeroing in on Solid Evidence (LOGOS)** Once you have introduced your topic you need to add facts, examples, and evidence to support your claim. Be sure that this does not confuse you - or the reader! Your body paragraphs should

Created by The Teaching Factor ©2017 *6-11 Steps from Revision Gameboard by @LisaGuardino*

FIGURE 3.9 Turn revision into a game: Students work around the board to edit and improve their writing.

Assistive Technology Tools

For students with diverse learning needs, there are additional technology tools that can help assist in writing and revising. For instance, Read&Write offers such writing tools as word prediction, dictation, and picture dictionaries. It also has a text-to-speech feature to read aloud what students have written, which can help with proofreading. Teachers and students can also use voice notes for peer review and teacher feedback. Available for all major mobile and desktop platforms, Read&Write is subscription based but does offer a free thirty-day trial.

Rubrics and Evaluation

I often get asked about the rubrics and evaluation I use to measure my students writing abilities and learning targets as defined by the Common Core State Standards. Because New York, my home state, publishes rubrics for middle-school essay writing and short response writing activity, I primarily use these. I share the rubrics with my students when I hand out an assignment or assessment, and together we go over the elements that I will be evaluating. For some educators, these rubrics can be limiting, and for students, abstract and unclear. As teachers, we want to be clear and articulate about the learning targets expected of our students and then think about how we can help our students achieve these goals. Not everything has to be graded, and sometimes the graded element creates anxiety and stress for students. In order to reduce the stress and anxiety of grades and graded work, I share with students lots of models and exemplars for us to examine together to understand the qualities of an essay that meets the learning standards.

When it comes to traditional writing assessments, most schools and states already have uniform, required rubrics for teachers to assess student writing. Additionally, the subscription-based platform, Turnitin, which many high schools purchase as an anti-plagiarism tool, offers a collection of rubrics for teachers to access, download, and utilize in its Feedback Studio. You can use the standard rubrics or even customize your own depending on what you are measuring. Blank rubrics and non-numerical rubrics are also available. I like

the Turnitin Revision Assistant tool: Students upload their writing, and the platform will edit and mark any grammar, usage, and mechanical issues.

Goobric is a good alternative to Turnitin if your school has Google Classroom. This Chrome extension helps simplify grading writing assessments on Google Docs and provides helpful evaluation tools. Goobric attaches a digital rubric to Google Docs documents so you can grade and comment on student work within a single browser tab. Basically, the attached rubric appears at the top of the student's assignment in Docs, you fill in the rubric with a few easy clicks, and then your individual comments and the rubric data are time stamped and appended to the bottom of the document for the student to view. Using these tools enables you to give students feedback in real time and helps make grading more efficient.

Key Points

Moving forward, think about how many essays your students are writing and whether they have opportunities to write and revise their writing. Students need opportunities to practice all types of writing to improve their communication skills in print and digitally, as well as their oral communication skills. Despite it being the backbone of academic writing, not every assignment that students write needs to be an essay. We want to help our students become solid writers who can effectively communicate no matter the format, genre, or product. The more students have the opportunity to write, revise, and craft their words in ways that articulate complex ideas, critical thinking, and problem-solving, the better they will become at producing clear and coherent writing where words become actions.

TABLE 3.1 Tools, Strategies, and Standards

Teaching Techniques & Strategies	Resources	Links	ISTE Standards for Educators and for Students	Common Core State Standards
Hochman Method	The Writing Revolution	thewritingrevolution.org	(E) 7a. Analyst Provide alternative ways for students to demonstrate competency and reflect on their learning using technology.	CCSS.ELA-Literacy.W.8.2.D Use precise language and domain-specific vocabulary to inform about or explain the topic.
Digital Mind Mapping Tools	MindMeister Popplet	mindmeister.com popplet.com	(S) 3d. Knowledge Constructor Students curate information from digital resources using a variety of tools and methods to create collections of artifacts that demonstrate meaningful connections or conclusions.	CCSS.ELA-Literacy.W.8.6 Use technology, including the Internet, to produce and publish writing and present the relationships between information and ideas efficiently as well as to interact and collaborate with others.
Writing Resources for Educators Online	Twitter Hashtags Two Writing Teachers Raising Readers and Writers Trail of Breadcrumbs	#tcrwp #2ndaryELA #teachwrite #engchat Twowritingteachers.org Raisingreadersandwriters.com trailofbreadcrumbs.net	(E) 1. Learner Educators continually improve their practice by learning from and with others and exploring proven and promising practices that leverage technology to improve student learning.	
Writing Platforms	Writable	writable.com	(E) 6b. Facilitator Manage the use of technology and student learning strategies in digital platforms, virtual environments, hands-on makerspaces or in the field.	CCSS.ELA-Literacy.W.8.4 Produce clear and coherent writing in which the development, organization, and style are appropriate to task, purpose, and audience.
Assistive Technology for Writing	Ginger Grammarly ProWritingAid Read&Write	gingersoftware.com grammarly.com/edu prowritingaid.com texthelp.com	(S) 6a. Creative Communicator Students choose the appropriate platforms and tools for meeting the desired objectives of their creation or communication. (E) 7a. Analyst Provide alternative ways for students to demonstrate competency and reflect on their learning using technology.	

continued

Teaching Techniques & Strategies	Resources	Links	ISTE Standards for Educators and for Students	Common Core State Standards
Rubrics and Evaluation	Self-editing and Peer Editing Checklist	tinyurl.com/przzgd5	(E) 7b. Analyst Use technology to design and implement a variety of formative and summative assessments that accommodate learner needs, provide timely feedback to students and inform instruction.	CCSS.ELA-Literacy.W.9-10.4 Produce clear and coherent writing in which the development, organization, and style are appropriate to task, purpose, and audience.
	Goobric for Google Chrome	tinyurl.com/jkz504r		
	Turnitin	turnitin.com		

Poetry
Traditional, Visual, Makerspace

In the introduction to his *Collected Poems*, Robert Frost wrote, "a poem begins in delight and ends in wisdom" (1939), which aptly sums up poetry's benefit to students. Poetry seems easy: Its words are often sparse on a page, and it can be an entry into writing for struggling or reluctant writers (and readers) because of its brevity. At the same time, that brevity can be deceiving. Less is more, and a poet is capable of using words to emphasize arguments, information, and autobiography. Poetry is a multifaceted tool that can provide students opportunities to reflect on literature, content-area subjects, and their own feelings and emotions, while increasing their understanding of the material being covered within classroom instruction. Poetry supports language and reading development because it brings aesthetic connections to topics and provides a personal relationship with content material. Sharing poetry with our students offers both delight and insight through the power of words.

In his article "Why Teaching Poetry Is So Important," Andrew Simmons (2014) wrote, "Poetry enables teachers to teach their students how to write, read, and understand any text." Yet poetry and creative writing tend to get the short end of the stick in secondary school. This chapter makes an argument for bringing them to the forefront of teaching reading and writing. Poetry and creative writing help students build writing skills, grow word knowledge, be creative, and apply learning in meaningful ways as creative communicators. In addition to offering fresh ideas for teaching budding writers about traditional poetry forms, this chapter will discuss ways to combine poetry with digital age skills—from using video production techniques to create visual poetry to hacking interactive poetry in a makerspace. As you'll see, immersing your students in *reading* and *experiencing* poetry across content areas exposes them to a variety of formats, genres, and topics. At the same time, this allows students to see the depth poetry offers and expand their understanding of poetry, which in turn will enrich their writing.

Introducing Poetry as Cross-Disciplinary Literacy

Poetry does not have to be taught, read, and written in English and reading classes only. Poetry works across the disciplines. What if a math teacher started the school year by asking students to write an ode to math or their favorite number? A poem in praise of the ordinary things in life, an ode can follow a specific rhyme scheme and stanza pattern, but does not have to. Think about asking your students to write an ode for a specific time or event in history, for a scientific concept, or to celebrate their favorite activity outside of school. You would learn a lot about your students from the latter. Once students write their own unique ode, they can share them on the free Flipgrid video discussion platform for others to listen and respond to.

Poetry and Science

Poetry can easily be tied to science, as well, and picture books and anthologies are great resources for read-alouds at the beginning of a lesson. For example, Sylvia Vardell and Janet Wong's *The Poetry of Science* (2015) covers all things science—from ecology to dinosaurs—in more than 250 poems by a wide variety of poets. Likewise, you can find many science-related poems on Poets.org, including "Dark Matter and Dark Energy" by Alicia Ostriker, which pairs well with an earth science or astronomy curriculum. Her description of dark matter "holding everything loosely together/the way a child wants to escape its parents/and doesn't want to" helps readers visualize how dark matter exists in space, clumping together what we can't see. You could even use this poem in conjunction with a video or an excerpt of Neil deGrasse Tyson's *StarTalk* podcast "Cosmic Queries: Dark Matter and Dark Energy." After listening to the podcast, students can synthesize their understanding by writing a poem. Students can use poems to further their understanding of a concept or write poetry to showcase their learning and new knowledge.

Dark Matter Poem

Dark Matter Podcast

Poetry and History

What if students created a found poem about the Declaration of Independence or a blackout poem based on a primary source studied in history class? To create a *found poem*, readers select and combine memorable words and phrases from a text to create or "find" a poem. Students can create their found poems after a text has been read, in part or in whole. Whether students use a textbook, article, or a piece of literature, found poems help them to understand the text deeply and make meaning by lifting the important words and phrases and remixing them in a more compact format. Similarly, *blackout poetry* uses words from another writer but remixes the words to shape a new poem, idea, or concept by "blacking out" the unnecessary words and phrases in the text. A blackout poem highlights the negative space of a poem to take new shape. Provide your students with examples for inspiration. Annie Dillard's *Mornings Like This* (1996) is a collection of found poems, for instance. A quick online search for the term *blackout poetry* will yield an array of beautiful poems that not only concentrate on the written word, but also are blacked out to form an image or use illustration that highlights the meaning of the text.

Lyrics are poems too. Lin-Manuel Miranda's blockbuster musical, *Hamilton*, retells the story of U.S. Founding Father Alexander Hamilton's life history through rap and other musical styles. Bringing a new perspective on American history that attracts a wide audience, the show's ingeniousness approach also provides inspiration for creative assignments: Imagine if students wrote a biography of another historical figure in lyric form.

The use of lyrics can also be adapted to other disciplines, as well. For example, I have seen English teachers set Shakespeare's *Romeo and Juliet* to modern music. Similarly, Jordan Allen-Dutton created the hysterical and award-winning *The Bomb-itty of Errors*, an adaptation of Shakespeare's *The Comedy of Errors* spoken in rap rather than Elizabethan English. Not to leave out science and math, these subject areas can take existing melodies and have students write songs or raps about solving a mathematical equation or the elements on the periodic table.

ACTIVITY: CHOPSTICK POEMS

Another unexpected place to find poetry is on chopsticks. Here's a quick lesson plan for using chopsticks to create poetry (Figure 4.1). You'll need:

o 2 or more sets of chopsticks per student

o Pen or fine tip marker

o Music of several genres and styles but without lyrics

OBJECTIVE: Practice poetry writing skills and descriptive vocabulary based on different music genres and styles.

PROCEDURE:

1. Distribute chopsticks to students.

2. Play a song for the class; instrumental music might work well. After the students listen to the song for a minute, instruct them to write a word, phrase, or image that the music evokes on one side of a chopstick. Repeat with different music styles until sides of all chopsticks are filled.

3. Have students line up their chopsticks and roll them under their hands to create new word combinations and poetry from the words on the visible sides.

4. Divide students into groups, so students can share their chopsticks and combine their words to create a group poem.

FIGURE 4.1 Students write prose on chopsticks to create a variety of poem options based on the words displayed on the specific chopsticks.

Visual Poetry Projects and Movie Making

Students need to read poetry if they are writing their own poems. An excellent tool for literary analysis and close reading exercises, poetry uses vivid language that paints a picture in the reader's mind. When my students are introduced to Shakespeare's sonnets, for example, we read many in class together to understand Shakespeare's language, meaning, and tone. I then divide students into small groups and assign each a sonnet for the Five Frame Photo Story activity: Students read, interpret, and summarize the sonnet in five original photographs. Using only images, students must showcase the main idea presented in the sonnet. When language is complex, visuals are helpful to support comprehension, thinking, and meaning making. (For more discussion of the Five Frame Story activity and its originator The Jacob Burns Film Center, see Chapter 2 of *Personalized Reading*.)

Another visually appealing poetry video project is The Sonnet Project from the New York Shakespeare Exchange. This organization is working to produce videos of all 154 of Shakespeare's sonnets. Each video highlights a specific location around the five boroughs of New York City as professional actors dramatize a sonnet. (The organization is now sponsoring international and U.S.-based versions of this original series, as well.) After viewing three or four different videos, my students and I discuss the visual choices the directors made to help viewers understand the meaning and interpretation of the sonnet. I then assign students a sonnet so they can create their own movie that visually showcases the sonnet's true meaning and key ideas. To help students analyze the sonnet and plan their movie, I give them a graphic organizer that breaks down the project into smaller parts and scaffolds their thinking. Some of our learners need this type of scaffolding for making meaning out of poetry, whether with complex texts like Shakespeare or a standard poem.

I present the graphic organizer shown in **Figure 4.2** to help students peel back the layers of Shakespeare's sonnets. In class, this would be an I Do, We Do, You Do lesson where I first model a close reading of a sonnet. I think aloud in front of the class, sharing my questions and inferences about the sonnet.

I might annotate the sonnet displayed on a SMART Board or under a document camera so students can see my interaction with the sonnet, as well. Then, I post another sonnet on the board, and together we read it aloud and examine it closely, trying to make sense of Shakespeare's words and meaning. This is an opportunity for students to articulate their questions and meaning making. We might reread the sonnet multiple times or chunk it into stanzas to summarize, outline, and synthesize. Lastly, I give students in small groups or independently a third sonnet to try on their own. This teaching formula is a gradual release for students becoming independent thinkers and readers of complex text.

For my ELL students or students with learning differences, I sometimes include a word bank with definitions under the sonnet. Additionally, I might ask them to draw a picture of the images that come to their minds as they are reading. Visuals are helpful for many learners. Resources, such as SparkNotes' No Fear Shakespeare site offer modern English translations of Shakespeare's texts that students can access for better understanding.

The most challenging aspect of Shakespeare for students today is his language. When students read Shakespeare, they often struggle to make sense of what he is saying because it is almost a foreign language for many. One way to help students to make sense of Shakespeare's language is to show them a few Pop Sonnets, which turn popular songs into Shakespearean sonnets, and have them figure out what contemporary song the sonnet is channeling. Pop Sonnets can be found on the Tumblr page popsonnet. tumblr.com or in Erik Didriksen's collection *Pop Sonnets: Shakespearean Spins on Your Favorite Songs* (2015). Similarly, in the *William Shakespeare's Star Wars* series of books, Ian Doescher depicts George Lucas' epic movies in Elizabethan English. These are fun to read or listen to and inspire students to think how they might remix one of their own favorite tales and transform it into a sonnet or poem. For these remix and Pop Sonnet assignments, I do *not* require students to write in Shakespearean English but do require students to modify the language to follow the sonnet rhyme scheme. An assignment like this is more complex for secondary students and again, a graphic organizer is helpful for students to draft their Pop Sonnets in the correct rhyme scheme to match Elizabethan English sonnet formula. Imagine what you might inspire if you assigned students to find a contemporary text and rewrite it into Shakespeare's Elizabethan English.

SHAKESPEARE SONNET CLOSE READING & ANALYSIS VIDEO ASSIGNMENT

SONNET 29	PARAPHRASE IN YOUR OWN WORDS
When, in disgrace with fortune and men's eyes, I all alone beweep my outcast state, And trouble deaf heaven with my bootless cries, And look upon myself, and curse my fate, Wishing me like to one more rich in hope, Featur'd like him, like him with friends possess'd, Desiring this man's art and that man's scope, With what I most enjoy contented least; Yet in these thoughts myself almost despising, Haply I think on thee, and then my state, Like to the lark at break of day arising From sullen earth, sings hymns at heaven's gate; For thy sweet love remember'd such wealth brings That then I scorn to change my state with kings.	**Word Bank** **Beweep:** lament; to cry over **Scope:** outlook or view

Summary	Figurative Language Devices

Tone & Mood	Theme
Sonnet 29 shows the poet at his most insecure and troubled. He feels unlucky, shamed, and fiercely jealous of those around him.	

FIGURE 4.2 To help students read and make sense of Shakespeare's Sonnets, I provide this graphic organizer. Sometimes I fill in some information to help students draw connections or nudge them to notice something specific in the text.

Listening and Spoken Poetry

With all the emphasis on reading and writing, we often forget that great stories and poems were meant to be heard as much as read. Listening to poetry read aloud helps readers and writers understand the complexity of compact words, bringing meaning to the forefront with rhythm, rhyme, pause, and emphasis. When we hear a poem, words come to life. **Table 4.1** highlights some of my favorite poems to listen to. (Please be sure to preview these before you share them to make sure they are appropriate for your students.)

Another good source for listening is the YouTube channel of Poetry Slam, Inc. (PSi). The PSi mission is to "promote the creation and performance of poetry that engages communities and provides a platform for voices to be heard beyond social, cultural, political, and economic barriers," leading to "a world where all persons have the ability to express themselves creatively through poetry using the power of voice" (n.d.).

RECITATION COMPETITION

Speaking and reciting poetry is helpful for students' understanding, and sometimes a competition is just the incentive students need to give it a try. Poetry Out Loud is a national program that promotes poetry through memorization and recitation. Students must memorize and present a poem of their choosing from the official Poetry Out Loud anthology, competing locally and, potentially, nationally with other high schoolers for cash awards. In partnership with the National Endowment for the Arts and The Poetry Foundation, Poetry Out Loud offers lesson plans, videos, recitation tips, and its poetry anthology online. In my district, the high school participates in Poetry Out Loud annually. Students prepare in class and then compete school-wide one afternoon in our media center. Some students have even gone on to compete at the state and national level. Holding a classroom or school-wide poetry reading showcases the spoken word as well as helps students understand the depth of each poem selected and presented for others.

TABLE 4.1 **Poems for Listening**

Poem	Poet	Reading Link
"And Still I Rise"	Maya Angelou	youtu.be/JqOqo5oLSZo
"Blink Your Eyes"	Sekou Sundiata	youtu.be/RRonTMg3kbs
"I Am NOT Black, You Are NOT White"	Prince Ea	youtu.be/qoqD2K2RWkc
"To This Day"	Shane Koyczan	youtu.be/ltun92DfnPY
"21"	Patrick Roche	youtu.be/6LnMhy8kDiQ

Imagine your students presenting their own spoken poetry or hosting a poetry slam for the school community. As Andrew Simmons explained, "Reading original poetry aloud in class can foster trust and empathy in the classroom community, while also emphasizing speaking and listening skills that are often neglected in high school literature classes" (2014). When students read poetry aloud, they gain a deeper understanding and are able to use tone, pause, and vocal variation to suggest meaning.

Give them opportunities to read their poetry aloud in the classroom or other settings. When I was a student, for example, my high school hosted monthly coffeehouse evenings. Our school cafeteria was transformed into a coffeehouse, and students would sign up to present, perform, and showcase their talents. There were bands playing, spoken word, song, and even stand-up comedy. With the lights dim and students gathered together after school hours, it showcased students' talents and passions as well as celebrated the arts. Allowing students the time to write their own poems for a poetry slam, school-wide event, or just for the classroom, can produce inspiring and moving outcomes.

Writing Poetry

Writing poetry builds on what students already know about language, words, and figures of speech. When writing poetry, students are developing their reading, writing, and thinking skills—all while playing with words, images, sounds, rhythm, and ideas. Poets present vivid pictures through sensory images, words that appeal to sight, hearing, touch, taste, and smell. Someone once told me that poems are like buildings, some are long and skinny, sometimes with only one word on a line. Others are wider with much longer lines. The choice is personal: Each writer has to decide how their poem should look and sound in order to convey their perspective and vision. Additionally, poets also think of the blank space and make decisions where to pause, stay silent, and leave something unsaid. Give your students the opportunity to try a variety of poetry formats and styles, such as:

✦ **BIOPOEMS** or **HISTOPOEMS** provide students with the opportunity to create a biographical or historical summary about a topic or person. Each line of a biopoem or histopoem has a prescribed focus, guiding students to summarize the information from a variety of perspectives. Biopoems and histopoems are great to use in social studies, science, and with literature.

✦ **BLACKOUT POEMS** are artistic creations that repurpose a text into a blend of words and images. Writers keep visible the words on a page to use and then black out or obscure the words that are not needed, sometimes with elaborate illustrations.

✦ **FOUND POEMS** are created by rearranging words from an existing text to create new meaning. Found poems are like word collages.

✦ **FREE VERSE** is a poem that does not follow any rhyme scheme, meter, rhythm, or specific form. There are no rules with free verse poems.

✦ **HAIKU** is traditional Japanese poetry that follows a specific format. These seventeen-syllable poems are often about nature and don't rhyme. Haiku's three lines follow a five-, seven-, and five-syllable pattern.

✦ **LIMERICKS** have strong rhythms and rhymed verses. These five-line poems are often funny or tell a joke. The Poetry Foundation identifies the rhyme scheme of limericks as "AABBA, in which the first, second and fifth line rhyme, while the third and fourth lines are shorter and share a different rhyme" (n.d.).

✦ **ODES** celebrate a person or thing and date back to antiquity. In Greek, *ode* means to sing.

✦ **SONNETS** come in many styles, but all typically have fourteen lines written in iambic pentameter. The rhyme scheme depends on the type of sonnet. For instance, Shakespearean sonnets have a rhyme scheme of ABAB CDCD EFEF GG across three quatrains (four lines in a group) and a couplet (two rhymed lines) at the end.

Artifacts and tangible items, such as photographs, objects, other poems or quotes, can inspire students when writing poetry. Students can model other poems, mimic examples, and write about their own observations, experiences, and memories. Writer Lillian Morrison pointed out, "Writing poetry can be a way of pinning down a dream; capturing a moment, a memory, a happening. It's a way of sorting out your thoughts and feelings" (as cited in

Fitch & Swartz, 2008). When students have a tangible picture or artifact, they can examine their subject the way an artist studies a subject for a painting: closely and critically, capturing the essence of the subject.

Often during my class poetry unit, I lead a lesson in which students try out multiple poetry forms and suggested topics. The important thing is for students to express themselves. I give students a series of topics to write from. Completing these poetry starters and seed ideas as a series of quick writing exercises generates a lot of ideas consecutively so that students have five or six quick starts for poems. The object of the lesson is not to create the perfect poem but just to capture some thoughts in writing. I don't expect students to finish a whole piece in the short time of doing the quick writes, but I hope they will produce a piece with potential that they might want to develop later in a writing workshop. **Figure 4.3** showcases many of these quick write prompts.

Say It, but Don't Really Say It Poem	Eve Merriam's poem "New Love" expresses love without ever using the word. How then do we know that she is talking about love? Have your students write a love poem (or a poem about anything) without including the word it's about.
Write Based on Another Poem	Have students write based on a mentor poem, responding to the author and images in the poem. For example, students could argue with the poem, or write about the memories or thoughts the poem evokes. Students could talk back to the poet by writing a letter sharing their story, experience, or argument.
"Tell All the Truth but Tell It Slant"	Emily Dickinson wrote, "tell all the truth but tell it slant." Students can write true statements about themselves and then "slant," or stretch, one truth. This is a spin off the icebreaker activity Two Truths and a Lie in which people write down two true statements about themselves and one lie; others in the group then have to identify the truths and the lie.
Hopes and Dreams Poem	In Mary Oliver's poem "The Summer Day," she wrote, "Tell me, what is it you plan to do with your one wild and precious life?" After reading this poem with students, use the last line as a challenge for your students to write down their life ambitions and dreams.
Shakespeare for 2019	Like the reverse of Pop Sonnets, this activity is about translating Elizabethan sonnets into contemporary poems. How would Shakespeare express his ideas if he were living in this day and time?

FIGURE 4.3
Quick write poetry activities help students develop possible poems and seed ideas.

These are only a handful of poetry quick writes that you can do with your students to produce seed ideas for poems. If we are going to develop the writing and critical thinking skills of our students, teachers "need to use a variety of strategies to plan, revise and strengthen their writing as they work independently and collaboratively with adults and peers to produce texts," in this case, poetry (New York State Next Generation Learning Standards, 2017).

Once students have a collection of poetry they can share their portfolio with others in creative ways. The idea is that the poems are not just written for the teacher but for a wider audience, an authentic audience. Students can use digital platforms to reach a global audience, such as through a blog, or can share poetry recordings in a closed space such as Flipgrid, or they can read their work at live events held in the school and community. Other possibilities include creating videos or narrated slideshows with iMovie, podcasts, dioramas, museum displays, or ebooks. Students could even pursue publishing their poems with online publications like *Teen Ink*, *Teachers & Writers Magazine*, and *Merlyn's Pen*.

Hacking Poetry In Makerspace

In high school, teachers mostly teach poetry as a close reading and literary analysis exercise. Some innovative teachers and media specialists are going a step further, however. They're using makerspaces and poetry in creative ways to help students not only develop an understanding of poetry, but also bring it to life.

Triggering Poetry

For example, Colleen Graves, a librarian, author, blogger, and maker extraordinaire, uses a hacking poetry project with her high school students that combines literary analysis and creative tinkering. *Hacking poetry* means that students create interactive poetry experiences using apps and makerspace materials. First, Colleen has her students select a poem that intrigues them. They read and analyze the poem by drawing the key images that are associated with poem. Having students create visual representations of the poem and the imagery in it requires them to think critically about the poem's meaning and symbolism. To visualize their poem, students can draw by hand or use digital tools, such as Sketchpad or Adobe Illustrator. Next, using Scratch, students record themselves reading their poem to convey meaning, mood, and tone. Then, students program Scratch to play the drawings and poem recordings when triggered. Once the recordings are complete, students attach the Makey Makey alligator clips to the computer and the conductive drawing, in order to trigger playback of the poems.

Makey Makey is an invention kit that allows users to turn everyday objects into touchpads and combine them with the internet using programs like Scratch. The Makey Makey Booster Kit contains a pen with conductive ink, so you can attach the Makey Makey alligator clips right to the student illustrations. (Or, students can just draw with pencils—the graphite in them can conduct electricity, too!) You can also use Circuit Scribe Maker Kit, which has a conductive silver ink pen for linking writing and drawing for more hacking poetry ideas.

Meanwhile, Colette Cassinelli has her students create interactive poster boards on the Harlem Renaissance. Students research an artist, poet, or writer and then showcase their analysis. Students produce a close reading analysis of three poems and create interactive displays with touch points or hot spots with Makey Makey. Students recorded themselves reading aloud the poems and sharing their analysis of the poems. When classmates touch a display board, they can listen to the student's research and poetry responses. The interactive poster board in **Figure 4.4** showcases a project from one of Cassinelli's high school students. The student compared Kendrick Lamar's music to Langston Hughes' poems. He offers an analysis of the two poets, and viewers can press buttons on the display board to hear Lamar's music and Hughes' poetry. The student also includes his own original poem.

FIGURE 4.4
Colette Cassinelli's high school students created interactive poetry posters with touch points that play the poetry aloud. (Image courtesy of C. Cassinelli.)

Self-Portrait Poetry

Another multisensory poetry project has its roots in a week-long poetry workshop I once attended with poet and author, Georgia Heard. Before we met, Georgia asked all participants to create a Self-Portrait Poetry Anthology, a collection of five or more poems that were a reflection or portrait of who we each were. We were to bring these poems and a brief reflection on why we chose each poem. I love this activity for students because it asks them to think about who they are and find poems that represent their multifaceted selves. Before we ask students to write their own poems, finding examples and models helps to introduce the genre and its range. What would be the poems that you select and why?

This assignment not only asks students to curate poems, but to also analyze the relationships and themes among the poems. Students have to determine the theme and articulate that theme as it connects with the poems selected. The work that students are doing for this assignment is literary analysis. Plus, it meets the Next Generation Writing Anchor Standards, to "develop personal, cultural, textual, and thematic connections within and across genres through written response to text and personal experiences" (2017).

Once students create their poem anthology, they can share it using digital platforms that bring student voice to the forefront. It's a great way to create a multisensory poetry experience.

Key Points

In *The Cloister Walk* (1997), Kathleen Norris wrote,

> *As children grow older and are asked to analyze poetry, they are taught that separating the elements in the poem—images, similes, metaphors— is the only way to "appreciate" it. As if the poem is somehow less than the whole of its parts, a frog students must dissect in order to make it live as if the purpose of poetry is to provide boring exercises for English class (pg. 60).*

In elementary school, students write poetry alongside the poems they read. Somewhere between middle and high school, poems become a text for students to read closely and analyze as Norris describes. Close reading and textual analysis are key literary skills, but not the only skills when it comes to reading and writing. We want students to see and hear the beauty and playfulness of words with poetry. Notice the deliberate choices writers make about what to say and the silences deliberately placed in poetry about specific events, concepts, and cross-curricular topics. Poetry has a place in all subjects to cultivate creativity in addition to learning and inquiry. Reading, writing, listening, speaking, and hacking poetry allows students to develop their creativity and flex their writing muscles.

Education should be a place where the need for diverse teaching methods and styles are valued, encouraged, and seen as essential to learning. In my own classroom, my aim is to build on students' learning and schooling and provide them with exciting and meaningful learning experiences that stir their curiosity and creative spirit. Poetry can do this and more. In the next chapter, we'll continue with more creative tinkering to broaden classroom writing.

TABLE 4.2 Tools, Strategies, and Standards

Teaching Techniques & Strategies	Resources	Links	ISTE Standards for Students	Common Core State Standards
Cross-Disciplinary Poetry	Poets.org Poetry Foundation	poets.org poetryfoundation.org	3. Knowledge Constructor Students critically curate a variety of resources using digital tools to construct knowledge, produce creative artifacts and make meaningful learning experiences for themselves and others.	CCSS.ELA-Literacy.W.9-10.2 Write informative/explanatory texts to examine and convey complex ideas, concepts, and information clearly and accurately through the effective selection, organization, and analysis of content.
Shakespeare	Five Frame Story *No Fear Shakespeare* Pop Sonnets The Sonnet Project	tinyurl.com/5FrameStoryboard sparknotes.com/shakespeare popsonnet.tumblr.com nysx.org/programs-2/sonnet-project	6. Creative Communicator Students communicate clearly and express themselves creatively for a variety of purposes using the platforms, tools, styles, formats and digital media appropriate to their goals.	CCSS.ELA-Literacy.W.8.4 Produce clear and coherent writing in which the development, organization, and style are appropriate to task, purpose, and audience.
Spoken Poetry	Flipgrid Poetry Out Loud Poetry Slam, Inc. (PSi)	flipgrid.com poetryoutloud.org poetryslam.com	6a. Creative Communicator Students choose the appropriate platforms and tools for meeting the desired objectives of their creation or communication.	CCSS.ELA-Literacy.SL.9-10.6 Adapt speech to a variety of contexts and tasks, demonstrating command of formal English when indicated or appropriate.
Hacking Poetry	Adobe Illustrator Circuit Scribe Makey Makey Scratch Sketchpad	adobe.com/products/illustrator.html sparkfun.com/products/13255 makeymakey.com scratch.mit.edu sketch.io/sketchpad	7. Global Collaborator Students use digital tools to broaden their perspectives and enrich their learning by collaborating with others and working effectively in teams locally and globally.	CCSS.ELA-Literacy.W.8.6 Use technology, including the Internet, to produce and publish writing and present the relationships between information and ideas efficiently as well as to interact and collaborate with others.
Publishing Poetry	*Teen Ink* *Teachers & Writers Magazine* *Merlyn's Pen*	teenink.com teachersandwritersmagazine.org merlynspen.org	6d. Creative Communicator Students publish or present content that customizes the message and medium for their intended audiences.	CCSS.ELA-Literacy.W.8.6 Use technology, including the Internet, to produce and publish writing and present the relationships between information and ideas efficiently as well as to interact and collaborate with others.

5

Writing, Robots, Makerspaces, and More

Making and STEM activities are popular today, and they do not have to be relegated to a particular space or subject area. In fact, making and STEM projects can coincide with the writing process and can help develop writing skills. Making is all about creativity and critical thinking—so is writing. Teachers around the globe are incorporating robotics and making to help support reading and writing. This approach to reading and writing allows students to participate in hands-on literary analysis and story building. This chapter discusses how makerspace projects can be presented in conjunction with writing to help boost student writing, collaboration, and communication skills. Yes, journaling and blogging about the maker process and projects are the traditional avenues for blending literacy and making, but there are a lot more options for innovative literacy—and you don't need a million-dollar, state-of-the-art makerspace lab to take advantage of them.

In this chapter, you will find a range of projects created by educators from around the globe. From no-cost recycled maker projects for puppet shows, to Legos and Play-Doh for stop motion animation and brainstorming for creative writing, to more expensive, complex robotics for coding and storytelling, maker tools can help students tinker with writing and thinking. At the end of the chapter, I include additional resources for makerspace curriculum, including grants and organizations that offer discounts and funding for makerspace materials. The chapter is organized by projects, tools, and complexity that can be added to elevate the writing process or stand alone. Making and tinkering supports students as design thinkers and creative communicators. As our digital world continues to evolve with multimedia, literacy and engineering are blended as a global initiative.

Low-Budget Makerspace and Writing Activities

When I was teaching a career exploration class, I gave small groups of students a shoebox filled with recycled items and things that others might throw away: packing peanuts, blank CDs, zip ties, coffee filters, even bottle caps. I told students that they had thirty minutes to create a prototype for

MAKERSPACE MOVEMENT VOCABULARY

Before your dive into STEM and writing activities, make sure everyone is clear on the terminology—and using it the same way. Depending on the teachers that you speak with, *makerspace* has different definitions; for some it is a class or a curriculum, whereas for others it can be an after-school club in the library or a supplemental project in the classroom. Here's a breakdown some key terms to help you understand the depth and variety of the maker movement as it is addressed in this chapter:

- **DESIGN THINKING** (or the **DESIGN LEARNING PROCESS**) is a hands-on approach to learning. Students brainstorm, collaborate, and prototype ideas and products that are solutions to problem-based learning. Teachers engage in problem-based learning experiences, and students use creative thinking and hands-on learning to build understanding and critical thinking.

- **CODE** is the set of instructions or commands used to control a device. A programming language is a type of code that is used to instruct a computer to perform specific actions.

- A **MAKERSPACE** is a place where students are able to make, create, and tinker on projects that can be tactile, virtual, or a combination of digital and tactile. A makerspace can be found in the classroom, the school library, a lab, or an after-school club space, depending on resources and budget.

- **MAKING** is the act of creating or inventing. There are companies that publish lesson plans and curriculum for making and makerspace projects, and there are others who believe that making is organic and driven by the students' interests and creative thinking.

- **PROGRAMMING** (or coding) is the act of writing instructions for a device to perform.

Students can program computers, robots, and other circuit-based tools, such as Raspberry Pi, Makey Makey, Ozobot Evo, and Sphero Bolt or Mini. Students can learn programming and code through such initiatives as Hour of Code, Scratch, and Codeacademy.

- **STEM** stands for science, technology, engineering, and math. This educational and career initiative launched by President Obama in 2011 encourages schools and students to pursue these fields for innovation and career readiness.

- **STEAM** stands for science, technology, engineering, art, and math. STEAM adds arts to the sciences and emphasizes the aesthetics and design elements required for engineering. Along with visual arts and digital arts, this also includes language arts and communication skills.

- **ROBOTICS** is the teaching, programming, and coding of robots in the classroom. Students make something tangible and then program it to perform actions. Lego has a robotics division, and some secondary students are building robots from the ground up. Smaller robots and circuits, from such companies as Ozobot and Sphero, are often used in schools to introduce students to engineering, programming, and robotics.

a new object that they would market to the world. Along with the recycled products in the shoe box, students had to complete a business proposal answering questions about the name of the item, cost to manufacture, price it would sell for, and how it would improve people's lives. This assignment brought to the forefront inventions that were thoughtful, sometimes silly, and always visionary. It was a hands-on building and writing assignment that required design thinking, collaboration, and inventiveness—but not a lot of funding or special equipment.

You do not have to get fancy with outfitting a makerspace or spend lots of money. Recycling provides lots of inexpensive and even free materials that you can use for creative writing or as a catalyst for a more formal writing assignment. Before you throw it away, think how someone else might repurpose it. Recycled objects might be used for designing puppets for which students write their own puppet show, for example. Or, students could create and write rules for their own games, following the example of *Caine's Arcade*, a documentary about a young boy who designed an interactive arcade out of cardboard boxes from his father's auto parts store in California. Is your classroom or household overrun with used bags? Watch *How to Make a PLARN Bed Roll* to learn how to crochet plastic shopping bags into sleeping mats for the homeless. In addition to students experimenting with recycled items, imagine them writing a children's book or feature article about their projects and their impact on the world. For a smaller writing project, students could write letters to local homeless shelters inquiring about the amount of donations needed and the intention to offer the mats to those in need.

Some projects just lend themselves to blending making and writing. One of my students was an amazing musician who wanted to work to build music appreciation with little kids for a class project. She contacted the public library and asked to teach a series of workshops for children ages four to six. At the librarian's request, she then outlined her ideas using one of my lesson plan templates. Each class included making instruments from recycled and upcycled materials: oatmeal tubs and coffee cans for drums, plastic eggs filled with dried beans for shakers, and so on. That summer, she presented her classes at the library with great success. From an educational point of view, this student was using communication skills, public speaking, researching, writing, and making. Clearly, this was an active learning opportunity in and outside of the classroom. Our students have great ideas, and as their teachers, we can help them facilitate their ideas to make something happen.

Legos and Play-Doh for Digital Animation and Storytelling

Writing and the writing process does not just have to be on paper written at a desk. Homemade modeling compound, store-bought Play-Doh, or building bricks such as Legos can be used to help facilitate storytelling and the writing process. These tactile tools are fun to use in any content area to showcase understanding, brainstorm writing projects, or even help writers think out ideas. Making and writing work together to help students tells stories, demonstrate, inform, and create something. For some, breaking out of the confines of a two-dimensional paper or from behind the computer screen is freeing and gets ideas flowing. Using modeling compounds and building bricks helps to transfer learning. Whether making or writing, students are creators and designers.

For example, in *Teach Like a Pirate* (2012), Dave Burgess described using Play-Doh on the first day of school to challenge students to create something that is important to them (p. 26). This hands-on activity helps build community in the classroom by learning about one another. Many teachers have adapted the Play-Doh Challenge to use it to help students communicate their ideas and interests.

Working with modeling clay or building bricks doesn't just have to be a one-time activity, either. Throughout the school year you can use Legos and Play-Doh in activities that build knowledge and evaluate understanding. Both toys are tangible items that can help students express their thinking. In my classroom, I use Legos to showcase reading and understanding of a chapter or the summary of a text. I often pull out a giant tub of the bricks and have students recreate scenes from the books we are reading. Think of this

activity as building a three-dimensional storyboard. In the movie industry, projects are storyboarded before going to film. A script is written or perhaps only outlined, and then the director sits with a storyboard artist to draw out the types of shots and how the story will play out visually. During this process the script is revised, edited, and sometimes pieces are added or omitted for length or purpose. As writers, we follow the same processes—sometimes with the artistic element and sometimes without. Drawing, building with Legos, and modeling with Play-Doh can help our visual learners outline their thinking and develop their ideas before and during writing.

In addition, Legos and Play-Doh can be brought out for brainstorming ideas and showcasing a concept in science, history, or math. Often in my classroom, we will have a challenge in which groups of students are given a short amount of time (five to ten minutes) to re-create a concept or answer a question using Play-Doh or Legos. (Simply forming the answer's letters is not allowed.) When time is up, we have a "gallery share" where we view the groups' creations and ask questions. This allows the creators to extend their thinking and clarify.

One of the seventh-grade science teachers in my school uses modeling clay for students to create a stop motion animation about the phases of mitosis. *Stop motion* is a film technique in which inanimate objects are posed, photographed, and re-posed repeatedly, replaying the sequence of captured images rapidly then creates the effect of movement. Students first learn about mitosis in class, create their own storyboard or outline of the process, and then begin modeling and capturing images for their stop motion videos. Students spend a week working in small groups during class time to re-create their storyboards in a modeling compound, taking pictures, and then editing the images into a video (**Figure 5.1**). For Macs and iOS devices, iStopMotion and the iStopMotion Remote Camera app can help you capture and create stop motion videos, or you can try Stop Motion Studio, which is available for creating on all major desktop and mobile devices.

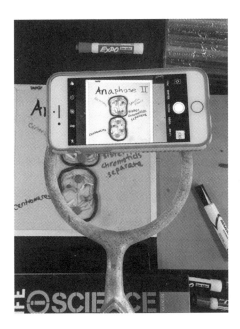 

FIGURE 5.1
After writing an outline or creating a storyboard, students produce stop motion animations to demonstrate mitosis in seventh-grade science.

Stop motion animations can be created in Google Slides, too, if you don't want to use tactile items and prefer working with digital images only. By making multiple slides and incorporating GIFs on the slides, students can make short animated videos to convey a science concept, illustrate how they solved a math equation, describe an event in history, and more. In **Figure 5.2**, I share the assignment page for a biography project my students made using Google Animations and screencasting.

Using a screencasting tool, such as Screencast-O-Matic, students can blend their stop motion animation with their voice-overs and musical interludes. Once the videos are completed, post online to share with others. Scan the QR code to view one of these student projects.

Based on your content area, grade level, or unit of study, this activity can be adapted and revised to best meet student needs. This is a great activity to use as an introduction to Genius Hour and Passion Projects. Or, it can be completed for a biography project for history, science, mathematics, or a side quest about great writers. You can create a checklist of items students should include in their video, including a key quote, symbolic images, and music to convey the theme.

Stop Motion Project

FIGURE 5.2

The Google Animated Stop Motion Video activity for middle-school students blends research, writing, and animation.

WHAT DOES GENIUS LOOK LIKE? GOOGLE ANIMATION VIDEO PROJECT

Choose a genius visionary that has inspired you: Albert Einstein, Thomas Edison, Steve Jobs, Elon Musk, Coco Chanel, J.K. Rowling, Martin Luther King, Jr., Walt Disney, Taylor Swift, Malala, Gandhi, or Shaun White.

Then, research and find out more about them: their education, their inspiration, telling quotes, and accomplishments. What characteristics do they have that makes them genius and a visionary? (A graphic organizer is provided for note-taking and student research.)

Create a Google stop motion animation movie showcasing this person, using images and GIFs After your stop motion animation slide deck is complete, write a script and describe the genius and visionary characteristics of this person. When your script is complete, you will screencast your description over the Google animation to create a stop motion animation movie.

The following directions to making a stop motion animation with Google Slides are adapted from Google Innovator Eric Curts' blog post "Stop Motion Animation with Google Slides" (2017).

1. **Create** your Google Slideshow as normal.

2. Insert **images**, **shapes**, **text**, and other items as needed.

3. To save time, **make copies of slides** and make small changes to the items on each slide to simulate movement.

4. To make certain slides last longer, make multiple copies of the slide.

5. When done, use the **"Publish to the web"** option to get **playable link** for your slideshow.

6. Adjust the "Publish to the web" link to **shorten the time between the slides** to make them appear animated (from 3000 to 2000 or 1000, depending on which speed which works best).

7. **Share** the link with others to view!

Small Budget Projects: Enhancing Stories Maker Tools

In Chapter Four, I shared poetry projects that used Makey Makeys and Scratch to become auditory and visual experiences. Similarly, such interactive maker tools as the Hummingbird robotics kit can elevate student writing and writing experiences to bring the words off the page for readers to now touch, hear, and interact with. As Colette Cassinelli explained in a blog post for *School Library Journal*,

> *Adding electronics and coding brings a new dimension to creative projects. The designer needs to pay special attention to how the user will interact with the project and requires students to think through the design process. Librarians can combine student's interests in making and electronics and use them for book talks, book character robots, reader's advisory, and classroom projects to support curriculum goals. (2018)*

Authors always have to think about their audience and purpose for writing and creating. With immersive technology, our experiences with text are interactive. When creating, students are not only thinking about their words, but they must also consider the audience, purpose, and design elements. Images and audio allow readers to experience text. These maker tools are a catalyst for writing and creativity that have endless possibilities, as Cassinelli suggested.

There are many ways to go about incorporating these interactive maker tools with writing. Some teachers have a set project in mind and then give parameters to their students for making (as with Chapter Four's poetry project), whereas other educators give their students the maker tools and allow open exploration and creation. Either way, using these tools is similar to the writing process: Students need to brainstorm what they are going to do or make and then outline their plans using design thinking. Outlining is an important part of both the writing and design process because it helps students to map out where they are going and necessary points that help to support a claim or prove a point. An outline is like a road map for the writer and designer. After outlining and drafting occurs, students undertake the revision process,

trying out their ideas and making any necessary edits and additions so that the arguments are clear and the design works smoothly.

A great introductory maker project that includes writing, making, and programming, the interactive poster in the previous chapter can be adapted to any subject. In math students could create a poster of interactive word problems then add a Makey Makey to the back to trigger the answer. In science, students could make models of the solar system or an organism, and in history, students could make an interactive poster about a famous historical figure or interactive timeline. Think about how writing can come to life by programming sounds and sound effects to emphasize mood and tone or important events. Students can write creatively, and then record sound effects to appear at certain points of the story as triggered by the Makey Makey. Remember those interactive reading books that allowed you to press a button and hear music or a sound effect? Students can make their own with Makey Makey. The story comes first, and then the sound effects are recorded and programmed after.

Enchancing with light rather than sounds, Chibi Lights from Chibitronics are circuit stickers that also help to make stories visually appealing and impactful. These lights enable you to blend circuits with creative writing and arts. I was introduced to Chibi Lights as an educational tool at ISTE's Annual Conference in 2017 when a librarian and media specialist shared a World War II interactive map she created using circuit stickers. With a press of one button, the Allied powers lit up on her map; pressing a second button highlighted the Axis powers. This sparked a flow of ideas about using circuit stickers in the classroom for creative and innovative activities, such as storyboarding, book creation, and more.

When I first started teaching in New York City, for example, my students created and illustrated their own children's picture books about an original hero myth they wrote as part of a unit on world mythology. If I were presenting the same lesson today, I would have students incorporating Chibi Lights and paper circuits to add another layer of a fun and interactivity to these stories. Within this assignment are opportunities for mini-lessons about characterization and word choice. Students need to decide which words or aspects of their illustrations they want to make light up for emphasis and theme.

Makey Makey and Chibi Lights introduce students to programming and circuits while at the same time flex their writing muscles. Whether the writing is creative or grounded in facts, these tools help words come to life and expand literary learning to incorporate more than reading, writing, speaking, and listening. For a total immersive experience with text, virtual reality (VR) and augmented reality (AR) can help students step into a storybook and soar beyond the words on a page.

Creative Writing and Virtual Reality

Learning doesn't only happen within the confines of the classroom walls. In fact, AR and VR break down the walls of the classroom to allow students to learn by suspending reality to travel in space, underwater, and to countries around the globe. Virtual reality companies are making more story-based virtual reality experiences that bring students into a place or take them back in time.

In *Personalized Reading* I mentioned TimeLooper, an augmented, virtual, and extended reality app that allows students to step into history and experience places and events in history around the world. These augmented reality field trip experiences allow students to immerse themselves in a time and place that could then be used for writing, reflecting, questioning, and guided learning. For example, with TimeLooper's Ambassador Program for educators, viewers can step into World War II to examine the multiple technologies developed during this time to determine whether these technologies were beneficial or detrimental to society. Immersing students into these experiences is more impactful reading than a textbook passage or viewing a movie because students are learning through experience. Combining all these layers makes for a deeper learning. Additionally, teachers can add writing prompts and open-ended questions or speech bubbles for students to answer and reflect to demonstrate their understanding. Virtual reality and augmented reality provide writing opportunities for students to showcase their learning and understanding.

Students can make their own story-based VR and AR experiences, as well. Using ZapWorks, Metaverse, and similar tools, students can be AR creators and storytellers. Zapworks is a platform that allows users to build and publish immersive AR experiences. This platform has many tutorials online to get started. Whereas Zapworks has a fee, Metaverse is a free augmented reality app that allows students to overlay characters, scenery, and animations into the physical world and interact with them. Metaverse has hundreds of ready-to-use, free learning experiences that have been created by teachers for teachers. No coding is required to make your own AR experience.

Big Budget Projects: Robots and Robotics

With STEM and engineering at the forefront of secondary school curriculums, students are building and programming robots in classes, in clubs, and for competitions. Robots can be made out of recycled products like cardboard or with a commercial kit, such as Mindstorms kits from Lego or a Hummingbird Bit kit from Birdbrain Technology, which consists of a customized control board, lights, sensors, and motors for students to program and

FUNDING STEM AND MAKERSPACE PROGRAMS

You do not necessarily have to pay out-of-pocket to provide the tools and technologies presented throughout this chapter! Many local and national grants are available to schools and teachers, including some from such corporations as 3M, Toshiba, and Lowe's. To see the range of possibilities, visit STEMgrants.com, STEMfinity.com, or GetEdFunding.com. All three websites list grants that provide funding, supplies, and equipment to support STEM and makerspace initiatives, while GetEdFunding also provides resources for grant writing. Competitions such as EngineerGirl and THINK are another resource, enabling students and teachers to apply for cash prizes, educational opportunities, and scholarships. In addition, some teachers use DonorsChoose.org, PledgeCents.com, or other crowdsourcing websites to reach out to vendors, local businesses, and parents to help fund tools and technologies for the classroom.

create. For a ready-made introduction to robotics, both Ozobot and Sphero offer small, programmable robots students can make light up and move while learning the basics of programming. The bigger and more expensive Cue, from Wonder Workshop, is a programmable robot that students can control through an app that allows them to create code in block-based visual languages (similar to Scratch) or text-based Javascript.

For example, Jessica Herring, an English teacher at Benton High School in Arkansas, uses Sphero robots in her English classroom. In one assignment, students choose a character from *The Adventures of Huckleberry Finn* and program Sphero robots "to represent the personality, emotions, and journey of that character" (Schwartz, 2016). As described in the article, "How Robots in English Class Can Spark Empathy and Improve Writing,"

> *To do this, students had to go back to the text and use close-reading strategies to find textual evidence that would back up their interpretation of the setting, motivations and feelings of the character. Then they had to decide how the Spheros [robot], a simple round ball that can light up, could represent those qualities. (Schwartz, 2016)*

The journey that the robots take around the classroom represents the journey of the characters in the book. In an assignment like Herring's, students work on layers of learning. They must design and create a story map using textual evidence, and then use code to give the robot a command to make it move in a specific direction. These layered tasks require mapmaking, programming, and students articulating the major events along the map that the robot follows.

Key Points

Writing a robot's program or designing a stop motion video is like the writing process—both require close reading, writing, and revising. It is not a one-and-done process, but one that requires close examination, trying out ideas, and playing back (and rereading) to then revise and edit for better meaning. In Shanda McCloskey's picture book *Doll-E 1.0*, tinker and coder Charlotte

receives what at first appears to be an ordinary doll as a present. Charlotte and her dog Bluetooth are unsure what to do with it, until she finds the doll's battery pack, then creative play and technology play collide. Like Charlotte in *Doll-E 1.0*, we can have students blend traditional literacy with high tech to create engaging, entertaining, innovative learning experiences that elevate learning and understanding.

Our students are knowledge constructors and innovative designers when engaged in makerspace activities. Robots and maker projects help students work on skills for the future as well as problem solving, collaboration, and design thinking. Robots do not have to be relegated to the math and sciences, but have a place across all disciplines. For example, I have seen high school students design robots to look like their favorite children's picture book characters, program the movements of the robot, and then record their reading of the book so that when the robot is hooked up to the computer it moves and recites the book for the audience. This activity involves making, reading, programming, speaking, creative thinking, and collaboration. To add writing, students can write an explanation of how the robot works, write a prequel or new ending to the robot story, or storyboard before getting started with making.

The future lends itself to a world of innovative literacy where students are working in mixed mediums to communicate, build, create, and problem solve. When given the opportunity to take risks, students develop, test, and refine prototypes as well as their own written ideas. Students are being asked to create innovative artifacts, take risks, and effectively express their ideas with different mediums. Schools are preparing young people for the changing landscape of the world and work. This chapter presented makerspace projects and ideas that "prepare [students] to thrive in a constantly evolving technological landscape" and meet the ISTE Standards for Students (ISTE, 2016). Moving forward, I look at the writing requirements for career fields and how you can bring them into your classrooms to help prepare students for the written requirements outside of school.

TABLE 5.1 Tools, Strategies, and Standards

Teaching Techniques & Strategies	Resources	Links	ISTE Standards for Educators and for Students	Common Core State Standards
Upcycling	*Caine's Arcade* *How to Make a PLARN Bed Roll*	youtu.be/faIFNkdq96U youtu.be/yr_WHW_tGSE	(S) 4c. Innovative Designer Students develop, test and refine prototypes as part of a cyclical design process.	CCSS.ELA-Literacy.W.8.7 Conduct short research projects to answer a question (including a self-generated question), drawing on several sources and generating additional related, focused questions that allow for multiple avenues of exploration.
Stop Motion Video Projects	HUE Animation Studio Lego Movie Maker app Minecraft Stop Motion app Stop Motion Movie Creator	huehd.com/animation tinyurl.com/legomovieapp education.minecraft.net tinyurl.com/stopmotionapp tinyurl.com/smmoviecreator	(S) 4a. Innovative Designer Students know and use a deliberate design process for generating ideas, testing theories, creating innovative artifacts or solving authentic problems.	CCSS.ELA-Literacy.W.8.2 Write informative/explanatory texts to examine a topic and convey ideas, concepts, and information through the selection, organization, and analysis of relevant content.
Makerspace and Programming	Chibi Lights Makey Makey Scratch	chibitronics.com makeymakey.com scratch.mit.edu	(S) 6b. Creative Communicator Students create original works or responsibly repurpose or remix digital resources into new creations.	CCSS.ELA-LiteracY.W.8.2 Write informative/explanatory texts to examine a topic and convey ideas, concepts, and information through the selection, organization, and analysis of relevant content.
Virtual Reality	*Inanimate Alice* Metaverse TimeLooper Timelooper Ambassador Program for Educators ZapWorks	inanimatealice.com gometa.io timelooper.com timelooper.com/educators zap.works	(S) 3d. Knowledge Constructor Students build knowledge by actively exploring real-world issues and problems, developing ideas and theories and pursuing answers and solutions.	CCSS.ELA-Literacy.W.8.3 Write narratives to develop real or imagined experiences or events using effective technique, relevant descriptive details, and well-structured event sequences.
Robots & Robotics	Cue Hummingbird Duo Lego Robotics Ozobot Robots Sphero Robots	makewonder.com/robots/cue hummingbirdkit.com lego.com/en-us/mindstorms ozobot.com sphero.com	(S) 4b. Innovative Designer Students select and use digital tools to plan and manage a design process that considers design constraints and calculated risks.	CCSS.ELA-Literacy.W.8.6 Use technology, including the Internet, to produce and publish writing and present the relationships between information and ideas efficiently as well as to interact and collaborate with others.

continued

Teaching Techniques & Strategies	Resources	Links	ISTE Standards for Educators and for Students	Common Core State Standards
STEM & Makerspace Funding	3M Gives	3m.com/3M/en_US/gives-us/education	(E) 2a. Leader Shape, advance, and accelerate a shared vision for empowered learning with technology by engaging with education stakeholders.	(Not applicable)
	DonorsChoose	donorschoose.org		
	EngineerGirl	engineergirl.org		
	GetEdFunding	getedfunding.com		
	Lowe's Toolbox for Education	toolboxforeducation.com		
	PledgeCents	pledgecents.com		
	STEMfinity	stemfinity.com		
	STEMgrants	stemgrants.com		
	THINK	think.mit.edu		
	Toshiba America Foundation	toshiba.com/taf		

Real-World Writing

*Writing Skills to Succeed
Beyond School*

If you ask students what they write in school, most often they will tell you essays. Essays are bittersweet: They can be eloquent but also rote, confining, and formulaic. Secondary schooling does not always have to be about essay writing. Throughout this book, I have shared academic writing assignments that go beyond essay writing to flex students' writing muscles. Once students leave school, they will have to use their verbal and written communication skills to succeed in what some people refer to as the real world. Students should have opportunities to try out these forms *before* they leave school. Whether you have students create resumes and cover letters, scripts for film projects, or written speeches across the content areas, try some of the suggestions in this chapter. Real life lasts much longer than the classroom, and our students need to be prepared.

Career and College Readiness

Prior to teaching eighth-grade English, I taught several middle-school electives, covering career exploration, speech and debate, drama, rock-and-roll history, and media literacy. Each course was grounded in literacy learning (reading, writing, speaking, and critical thinking) but focused on the specific theme. For instance, the career exploration class was designed to help students focus on real-world skills, such as exploring career options and developing financial literacy. I arranged weekly guest speakers to talk with the students about their line of work and career path. Listening to the senators, authors, nurses, doctors, fashion designers, and movie makeup artists was fascinating for my students, and there was always an opportunity for the class to ask questions, as well.

At the culmination of that semester, I gave students a writing assignment—but *not* simply an essay on their future careers. Instead, they had to write a cover letter and resume for themselves fifteen years into the future. The resumes needed to include objectives, employment history, and schooling. Underneath each section, students included bullet points to detail the skills and accomplishments they hoped to fulfill. The resume templates in Google Docs and Microsoft Office were great guides for students to begin, and every day I shared sample resumes from friends and family. This allowed students to see different styles and formats and choose the one that best fit their tastes. In addition, I taught each aspect of a resume in a series of mini-lessons.

Resume writing is a challenging task for many. Practice in resume writing and formal letter writing helps secondary students to highlight their strengths and articulate their goals. Students need opportunities to build these written artifacts for job applications, college, and career growth. Whereas this is not a writing exercise in endurance as an essay or longer writing assignment might require, resume writing requires students to synthesize career information and market themselves succinctly.

An even more succinct self-marketing strategy is the elevator pitch, which is like a short, verbal commercial about yourself. By short I mean thirty seconds or less, the average time it takes for an elevator to go from the ground floor to the top of a tall building. In an elevator pitch, a person communicates who they are, along with the skills and strengths they could bring to a company. After students complete their resume and cover letter, working on their elevator pitch can help students hone in on their verbal communication skills. I often invite guests in for mock interviews with the students and to listen to the elevator pitches. Drafting an elevator pitch can be just as challenging as writing a resume and cover letter. It needs to be persuasive while at the same time not come off as too conceited or pushy. Students must find the right balance when writing and presenting their speeches. In *Street Smarts: Beyond the Diploma* (2011), Jim Randel outlined the keys to a good elevator pitch:

1. *Short and to the point. 30 seconds tops.*

2. *Give the "headlines." What makes your story compelling?*

3. *Update you pitch periodically with new and interesting facts.*

4. *Deliver your pitch in a light-hearted tone. The elevator pitch is just an introduction—don't take it too seriously.*

5. *End with "I would love to tell you more if you have the time." But don't push. Let the listener decide what else he or she wants to know (Lesson 4).*

An elevator pitch is a narrative assignment that requires writing and speaking. Students need to craft their speech and deliver it with passion and energy to promote themselves and not turn others away. Students can share their elevator pitches on a video platform, such as Flipgrid, and give each other feedback to help revise their pitches to be stronger.

Storytelling and Personal Narratives

We live in a visual- and audio-saturated world. For some, listening to a great book can be just as inviting as reading words on a page. (I personally cannot commute to work without a book playing on my Audible app.) We want students to listen to great stories. Better yet, we want our students to craft their own stories that delight listeners. Public speaking, storytelling, and filmmaking are all genres that require writing. Instead of taking a test about an animal habitat, why not have students write a script and create a movie that demonstrates understanding of the subject under investigation? After reading Martin Luther King, Jr.'s famous speeches, students could write a speech about their own dreams using the rhetorical devices Dr. King used so eloquently. There are many different creative writing avenues that meet the Next Generation Writing Anchor Standards and help learners develop the skills of creative communicators.

The Moth
Radio Hour

To help you incorporate storytelling into your classroom, you can find help from moths—or at least The Moth. Dedicated to highlighting personal narratives and storytelling of ordinary people, The Moth is the organization behind *The Moth Radio Hour*, *The Moth Podcast*, and The Moth Education Program. If you have never heard *The Moth Radio Hour*, listen to Micaela Blei's "Life and Death on the Oregon Trail" (scan the QR code). Based on how the former teacher describes the Live Action Role Play (LARP) on Westward Expansion that she created for her third-grade students, you will probably wish you'd been in her classroom. Her story contains elements of humor, suspense, and conflict.

The Moth Education Program provides a framework and resources for eliciting stories and personal narrative with students. In addition, summer workshops in New York City are available for teachers to learn more about the framework and techniques for teaching the art and craft of storytelling and story writing. In the workshop I attended, for example, lots of oral drafting occurred in small groups before we ever put pen to paper. For reluctant writers, oral storytelling is one way to begin building their writing skills. Articulating our stories and ideas before committing them to writing is a planning process and prewriting strategy. As teacher and Moth Curriculum Partner Tara Zinger stated, "Hearing a laugh or a gasp from a peer can be just what a student needs to know they are on the right track, and that just doesn't happen as easily with a more traditional writing process" (Blei & Zinger, 2017).

Narrative writing is part of the New York State Next Generation Standards under the production and range of writing for middle-school students. Specifically, standard 8W3 states, "Write narratives to develop real or imagined experiences or events using effective techniques, relevant descriptive details, and clear sequencing" (2017). Writing and producing personal stories is about being honest and carefully considering structure, word choice, and description in order to share what matters. Writers must first identify the story and then make it compelling. The Moth Storyteller Micaela Blei shared five techniques of storytelling and what makes a story compelling:

- ✦ **CHANGE:** *Change is what separates a story from an anecdote. From the beginning to the end of the story, you're somehow a different person, even if in a small way.*

- ✦ **STAKES:** *We like to define stakes as what you have to win or lose in the story. Or, alternatively, what* matter*ed* to you?

- ✦ **THEMES:** *Choosing a theme can help a storyteller decide how to shape this particular story. Deciding what thread or theme you want to draw out for this particular five-minute version can help you make critical choices of details that pertain.*

- ✦ **SHOW VERSUS TELL:** *A story is most effective when you have at least one really vivid scene with sensory details, action, dialogue, and inner thoughts/feelings.*

- ✦ **BE HONEST/BE REAL:** *There's no one right way to tell a story. Be yourself. (Blei & Zinger, 2017).*

Storytelling, like speechwriting, requires students to write a script of what they are presenting to an audience. Both require elements of story, information, narrative, and oftentimes persuasion. Whereas storytelling is driven by a narrative story, for a speech, a story element can help connect with the audience and build credibility. When students are presenting speeches that are informative or persuasive, research, writing, and author's purpose are necessary.

Public Speaking and Speechwriting

We want our students to not only be able to write arguments, literary analysis, and research reports, but to write personal narratives that are engaging and descriptive, and that convey complex ideas and information clearly. This can be in the format of speeches, storytelling, and podcasts.

In my speech and debate class, students have to write and present many types of speeches to develop verbal and intellectual skills. The first half of the class focuses on public speaking. Students are introduced to the techniques used by great speakers in history, including John F. Kennedy and Martin Luther King, Jr., and then write and present three speeches: informative, persuasive, and narrative. In the second half of the course, students conduct research based on controversial topics in current events and participate in two debates. Depending on current events, the speech topics change each semester. Considering this is a middle-school class, it is an intensive writing class because students are writing, editing, and presenting daily. This helps students build writing skills, as well as learn elements of successful speech writing and public speaking. Speeches are drafted in class and then presented live for the classroom audience.

Speech Writing
HyperDoc

To incorporate speechwriting into your own classroom, consider modeling the assignment partially illustrated in **Figure 6.1**. (For the assignment's full HyperDoc, scan the QR code.) Students had to complete three mini-units in the HyperDoc to earn badges and showcase their learning and understanding.

SPEECH & DEBATE BADGE CRITERIA

Instructions: Use this document to ensure you have completed all of the required work to earn the following three badges. Your mastery of these three badges shows your strengths and skills as a public speaker. After completion of all the required work, and upon review and allocation of these three badges, students will earn an A in Speech and Debate for the quarter.

Task(s)	Expectation(s)
"Great Speakers Are Made, Not Born" — **Badge Criteria**	You are required to complete a series of reflections for this badge. For each post that has a video/website/book/ebook as media, include an APA or other citation at the end of your reflection. Below are the expectations for the reflections: **#1: Speech and Debate Reflection Google Form** **#2: Great Speakers in History** 1. Watch the videos of "I Have a Dream" by Martin Luther King Jr. and President John F. Kennedy's Inaugural Speech Transcripts: MLK's Speech and JFK's Speech 2. Write a reflection paper (2–3 pages) in which you address the bullet points below. Use this graphic organizer to help organize your ideas. • Summarize the key ideas presented in each speech and the rhetorical devices used in each speech to make these iconic speeches. Use direct textual evidence (3–4) to support your claims. • Write a paragraph about the speakers themselves. What strategies do MLK and JFK emulate in their public speaking? Identify four or more public speaking strategies using direct textual evidence to support your claims. • What makes MLK and JFK "Great Speakers?" Reflect on the elements of these speakers and their speeches that you hope to emulate this semester in Speech and Debate. Use specific details and examples. These will, in turn, be your personal speaking goals for the semester. **#3: Who is a "great speaker" of our time?** 1. Identify a speaker today who you think emulates the qualities of great speakers you identified in JFK and MLK. 2. Find a video that showcases this speaker, and include the video link that highlights the elements of public speaking utilized by this person. Post this video on Google Classroom for all to view, reflect, and review. (Select a video that is 3–10 minutes in length). 3. Write an analysis (1–2 pages) describing the strategies and rhetorical devices presented by this speaker. Use direct textual evidence to support your claim. Include specific information describing the aspects of this speaker you aspire to when speaking in public. Use this graphic organizer to help you organize your thoughts. **#4: Public Speaking Content Curation** • Using one of the following content curation/social bookmarking sites—Pinterest, ThingLink, or Symbaloo—find nine or more (9+) research and public speaking videos (3), research articles (3), and interviews with public speaking teachers or figures (3). • Annotate what can be found at each site and/or video and highlight one (or more), key quotes and a strategy for public speaking highlighted in the resource. • Describe in 2–3 sentences how this content can help you to be a better public speaker.
Request Feedback from Teacher	• I have completed all activities on Google Classroom. • I have linked my work when requested. • I have received peer feedback in the form of sidebar "comments." • I have submitted my work on the Great Speakers Are Made, Not Born Form. • I have shared my criteria document to Dr. Haiken with permission to either edit or comment.

FIGURE 6.1 This HyperDoc includes assignments for a speech and debate class unit on elements of effective public speaking. All student work was completed on Google Classroom.

Filmmaking and Screenwriting

In the age of the Common Core State Standards, teachers are asking students to "mine the text for details, ideas, and deeper meanings" (Fisher & Frey, 2014). Just as print text is layered with words, images, inferences, and evidence, so is film. If students are to develop deep understanding of texts, teachers need to model close reading skills to film too. In my media literacy course for seventh and eighth graders, we focus on visual literacy and watch many films together, reading and viewing them closely like any written text. Along with studying these models, writing and creating films is a big part of student work.

When watching a film, students should view for content analysis and understanding, but also to understand the filmmaker's point of view and purpose. In class, we discuss and examine the types of shots, match-on-match transitions, diegetic sound (any sound that originates in the film), and nondiegetic sound (sound that doesn't originate in the film but is added during the editing process, such as sound effects, narration, or musical score). We look at the use of music, color, and homages to other films and directors. Students learn about film tropes and characterization. The Jacob Burns Film Center (JBFC) provides a Visual Glossary on its website with terminology relating to film and media, offering not only definitions but also film clips to illustrate the concepts. By learning these terms, applying them to the creation process, and naming the movies that they are making, students not only build disciplinary vocabulary but also their sense of possibility expands. When analyzing film or creating a media text, we want students to understand that a filmmaker makes deliberate choices to convey a message or emotion the way an author selects specific words to convey meaning. This element relates to craft and structure as identified in the Common Core State Standards.

Crafting Fiction Films

The students' culminating project is to write a script and produce a film for a larger audience. As fans of *Stranger Things*, one class and I focused on suspense and the elements of suspense. First, we deconstructed the work of master suspense filmmakers, such as Alfred Hitchcock, and then students wrote the script for their suspense story, storyboarding the types of shots necessary to convey the plot, conflict, and characterization. Lastly, students went into movie-making mode.

Creating is a digital age skill, and the creation process is just as important as the final product. When students are creating film projects and writing their own scripts, designing the set, and making choices about lighting, sound, and editing, they are demonstrating critical analysis, creative collaboration, and multimedia communication. For ideas of projects that use these skills beyond full-scale movies, see the sidebar "Visual Writing Projects."

Writing a script for a film has its own specific format and requirements. Like writing any good story, when creating a movie, students need a beginning, middle, and end. Most importantly the story needs conflict to drive it. Students have to create authentic characters that viewers empathize with. It all begins with one thought, a seed, a spark, an overheard conversation, and an idea is born. Yet a writer or filmmaker cultivates the idea, outlines, drafts, and sketches the paths where the idea is to expand to reveal a story. Students need to outline and sketch their ideas like real writers and artists. Storyboards are great scaffolding tools to help students put their ideas down on paper and unravel the threads of ideas that encompass their story.

When students get stuck writing and creating, we look at how other films address similar ideas. When my students were trying to convey a sense of time in their movie, we looked at how Disney Pixar's *Up* (2009) uses time-lapse to show the passage of time: Every morning Carl's wife Ellie straightens his tie before work. To depict their long life together, the shot zooms in on one tie, then fast forwards through a sequence of many ties to suggest years passing, until the camera pans out and Carl and Ellie are elderly. (Scan the Time-lapse Example QR code, and fast forward to the 2:17 mark to watch this scene.) Watching this clip together helped my students think about how they might show time in a film.

Time-lapse Example

VISUAL WRITING PROJECTS

Here are more filming options you can do with your students in one or two class periods to building their visual literary and writing skills:

○ **BOOK TRAILERS:** I often have students make a book trailer for their favorite book. Any good preview needs a balance of words and images to invite others to read the book.

○ **CHARACTER MUSIC VIDEOS:** When my students read Agatha Christie's *And Then There Were None*, they work in small groups to select a character from the text, choose a theme song for that character, and create a music video to convey his or her characterization. If your students are musically inclined, you might even assign students to create their own song that represents the character. This blends creative writing and filmmaking.

○ **ART COMES TO LIFE:** Inspired by a wordless picture book, students use an image from Chris Van Allsburg's *The Mysteries of Harris Burdick* as a catalyst to create a video that expands on the mystery of the picture presented in the book. Students can choose between making a silent film or one with dialogue.

○ **FILMS GENRE PROJECT:** I often give my students choices with the projects they create in my classroom. When students are studying Shakespeare, I give them the option to present a scene as a silent film, rap, or musical. You can have students reenact a scene using any film genre.

○ **TED TALKS:** We all watch them. Have your students create a short TED talk about their own passion and interests. Sir Ken Robinson's "Do Schools Kill Creativity?" (2006) offers a catalyst for students to craft their own TED talk on how to make their school a better place.

○ **PREZI SCREENCASTS:** Students create a presentation using Prezi or Microsoft PowerPoint and then screencast themselves giving the presentation.

These informational texts could be used to teach, inform, or narrate content.

○ **LEGO MOVIES:** My son is obsessed with Legos, which inspired me to ask him to help me create a Lego version of a few scenes from *A Midsummer Night's Dream*. We took still pictures of various Lego scenes and screencast the images and text together. Your students could do the same with any poem, book, or play. (See Chapter 5 for more about how much fun Legos can be as a teaching tool to spark creativity.)

○ **COMMON CRAFT VIDEOS:** I love the ideas and images presented in many the Common Craft videos. Technically, these are screencasts of illustrated presentations. You can have your students create Common Craft–style videos on their own or using the Common Craft Cut Outs. You can sign up for a free pack of twenty-five Cut Outs online or pay a fee to access the complete library available on Common Craft.

○ **INTERACTIVE ADVENTURE VIDEO:** YouTube has a feature that allows you to link videos within videos. In the past, my students created a series of videos that analyzed critical theories of gender, race, and class in Disney animation. We linked all the videos together, allowing viewers to choose customized paths for learning or investigation. The same could be done with story flow if students write a branching story with multiple paths to different endings, similar to the *Choose Your Own Adventure* series of novels.

○ **STOP MOTION ANIMATION:** As detailed in Chapter 5, there are so many possibilities for students to create a stop motion animation to explain a concept, continue a story, and more.

For more sources of inspiration, try the *Anatomy of a Scene* video series from *The New York Times*. Found on the newspaper's website, the series presents analysis of current movies by having a film's director or producer talk through a scene and the decisions behind it. These short clips showcase types of shots, locations, special effects, and lighting and sound choices. The *Anatomy of a Scene* videos are helpful models and teaching tools for students to craft their own films and borrow film techniques from filmmakers today. Using movies as a teaching tool helps students grasp various concepts and ideas. Think about how you can use movie clips to help teach point of view, structure, and more.

Documentary Films

Researching to build knowledge is also a core skill, and creating documentary films is a creative way to give students practice. Writing different text types and for different purposes is a requirement for students to be college and career ready. When I came across the Op-Docs, short documentary videos on *The New York Times* website, I knew I had stumbled on a teaching tool gem. As its website states, Op-Docs are "documentaries, most under 15 minutes, that touch on issues like race and gender identity; technology and society; civil rights; criminal justice; ethics; and artistic and scientific exploration" (2018). These short films showcase aspects of life that are hidden or unspoken. For instance, *San Quentin's Giants* is an intriguing documentary about the San Quentin prison baseball team that showcases how baseball is a vehicle for reform, reflection, and purpose for the players. Whereas San Quentin uses storytelling and interviews, the Op-Doc *A Conversation About Race* features individuals talking about race and racism. This documentary can be used as a catalyst for classroom discussion or a project: What would this same conversation look and sound like in school from the students' perspectives?

San Quentin's
Giants

After watching a number of these Op-Docs with my students and discussing the research and filming elements involved, I ask students to research and investigate the issues that are worth shedding light on. Some students addressed bullying, whereas another group researched video game playing and addiction

among young people. In completing this documentary project, students had to gather relevant data from multiple sources, assess the credibility and accuracy of each source as with any research project, and integrate the information in documentary film writing. This led to conversations about bias and author's purpose. We addressed the danger of a single story, the importance of presenting multiple voices throughout the documentary, and the need to look at the different arguments surrounding their topic. After the research was conducted, students had to decide how they wanted to string together the facts. We looked at the differences between TED Talks, which are straightforward lectures, and Op-Docs, which blend a bit of narrative with information and argument writing through visual storytelling. On paper and in writing, students can use documentary filmmaking to make insightful arguments, illuminate different perspectives, and analyze a subject. When we add a visual emphasis with filmmaking, the writing and arguments are elevated. Students' attention to detail is expanded and literacy concepts developed.

Video and Filmmaking Tools

The two tools that my students and I use most often for creating videos are iMovie and WeVideo. Free for MacOS and iOS devices, iMovie enables students to use iPads to record and edit video. Available in free and paid subscriptions, WeVideo also has some really cool multimedia editing tools, green screens, and templates that teachers and students can use to create film and video projects. For example, an actor can shrink themselves for a special effect. If you're filming in school and need a specific background, use one of the templates or consult the lesson plans available in the Resource Hub on the WeVideo website. If you are a Google school, WeVideo synchronizes with Chrome. Green Screen by Do Ink is another video-making tool that is popular in elementary schools. Available for iOS devices for a fee, Green Screen enables you to create videos and choose a background to composite in behind the scene.

Global Connections and Opportunities

Student writing and creations are meant to be shared, and what better way to share them than through global collaborations? The ISTE Standards for Students identify global collaboration as one of the tenants of digital literacy and citizenship. Global collaborators are "individuals who use digital tools to broaden their perspectives and enrich their learning by collaborating with others and working effectively in teams locally and globally" (ISTE, 2016). Students can collaborate in the creative process by using collaborative technologies to share and produce content.

Blogs are simple and easy to create today and a great way to share student work. With web platforms like WordPress, Wix, and Kid Blogs, students can create forums, post their writing, and get feedback from their peers locally and globally. If you're not ready to go global, Edmodo and Flipgrid have the ability to hold collaborative conversations and share writing in a private or closed space only accessible to a project's participants. Check your school's technology policy, and be sure to choose the platform that complies with your district's requirements.

Many organizations help students partner with schools around the world to participate in collaborative projects. The Interactive Educational and Resource Network (iEARN-USA), for example, connects students around the world to promote cultural understanding and learning. iEarn also has one hundred projects that meet the Common Core State Standards and align with the United Nations Sustainable Development Goals. There are projects that include exchanging holiday cards or having students conduct research to showcase their learning with students around the world. ePals is a global collaborative network for pen-pal exchanges and collaborative projects. Part of Cricket Media, which publishes award-winning children's magazines, ePals pairs educators and students around the world for project-based learning, language learning practice, and cultural exchange.

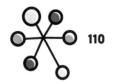

Flat Connections is a third global collaborative network and one that I have worked with in the past. The projects with Flat Connections include students working together to research and present their findings. My students have participated in both the Digiteen Project and the Horizon Report. Digiteen is a global collaborative project that has students examine digital citizenship across schools and countries. Students work in heterogeneous groups to look at what it means to be a responsible digital citizen. Students research aspects of digital citizenship and then write a collaborative report to share their understanding. Students also create an actionable educational project to promote effective digital citizenship at their local schools and in their communities. My students went into health classes in our middle school and taught their peers positive digital citizenship. As the Flat Connections Teacher Guide for the Digiteen Project states, "The purpose of the project is to educate on and promote effective Digital Citizenship and responsible online choices as well as immersing students into an online educational community for learning and collaborating" (n.d.). Before any collaboration, students write introductory blog posts to get to know one another because they are working across schools, across states, and around the globe. It is a mixed group of students in grades eight through high school.

Flat Connections harnesses the ISTE Standards for Digital Citizen and Global Collaborator (2016). Ideally, we want all our students to act responsibly and in a positive way when they interact with technology and digital spaces. These global collaborative projects allow students to practice positive, safe and ethical behavior online. Students are writing and working with others to produce a clear and informative report. Students need opportunities to collaborate and form positive interactions online. This, in turn, allows them to contribute constructively and explore global issues.

Another collaborative project through Flat Connections is the Horizon Report. Students read, research, and report about the current Horizon Report, published by The New Media Consortium. This report presents the present and future trends of technology at the current time, five years from now, and ten years into the future. Heterogeneous groups across schools in and outside of the United States work together to research and present one of the technology trends in an online report and presentation. Participating in this project allows students to learn from others about access to technology across the globe and where their own schools can make improvements with educational technology. Participating in global collaborative projects expands students' world view when they work with others to examine a topic like technology trends. As the 2017 Horizon Report states, "It is clear that there need to be more robust ways to assess student learning, assessments that go beyond standardized test scores and instead focus on the concepts, skills, and abilities students need to master in order to be successful when they start their careers" (p. 5). Global collaborative projects like the ones Flat Connections provides help to meet these goals and includes students in solving global issues.

Key Points

It is our responsibility as educators "to empower student voice and ensure that learning is a student-driven process" (ISTE Standards for Students, 2016). This requires teachers to expand writing across disciplines and include opportunities for students to use technology to be innovative communicators of their ideas, questions, and creations. Outside the world of school, most of our students will not be writing essays, lab reports, and document-based questions beyond secondary school and college. Offering students writing that is grounded in life skills and formats that we see in our everyday lives like blogs, filmmaking, and storytelling bolsters and excels students' literacy skills. Teachers must be creative and innovative with opportunities that go beyond traditional writing assignments, and offer more choice and access to digital technology that enables students to be creative communicators and advanced thinkers.

TABLE 6.1 Tools, Strategies, and Standards

Teaching Techniques & Strategies	Resources	Links	ISTE Standards for Students	Common Core State Standards
Narrative Story Writing and Storytelling	Audible The Moth	audible.com themoth.org	6d. Creative Communicator Students publish or present content that customizes the message and medium for their intended audiences.	CCSS.ELA-Literacy.SL.8.6 Adapt speech to a variety of contexts and tasks, demonstrating command of formal English when indicated or appropriate.
Public Speaking	TED Talks	ted.com	6c. Creative Communicator Students communicate complex ideas clearly and effectively by creating or using a variety of digital objects such as visualizations, models or simulations.	CCSS.ELA-Literacy.SL.8.4 Present claims and findings, emphasizing salient points in a focused, coherent manner with relevant evidence, sound valid reasoning, and well-chosen details; use appropriate eye contact, adequate volume, and clear pronunciation.
Filmmaking	Do Ink iMovie Jacob Burns Film Center Visual Glossary *The New York Times* Op-Docs *The New York Times* Anatomy of a Scene WeVideo	doink.com apple.com/imovie tinyurl.com/visualglossary nytimes.com/ 2018/04/30/ opinion/about-op-docs.html nytimes.com/column/ anatomy-of-a-scene wevideo.com	6c. Creative Communicator Students communicate complex ideas clearly and effectively by creating or using a variety of digital objects such as visualizations, models or simulations.	CCSS.ELA-Literacy.W.9-10.3 Write narratives to develop real or imagined experiences or events using effective technique, well-chosen details, and well-structured event sequences.
Global Collaboration	Edmodo Epals Flat Connections iEarn Kid Blogs WordPress Wix	edmodo.com epals.com flatconnections.com us.iearn.org kidblog.org wordpress.com wix.com	7a. Global Collaborator Students use digital tools to connect with learners from a variety of backgrounds and cultures, engaging with them in ways that broaden mutual understanding and learning.	CCSS.ELA-Literacy. SL.9-10.1 Initiate and participate effectively in a range of collaborative discussions (one-on-one, in groups, and teacher-led) with diverse partners on grades 9–10 topics, texts, and issues, building on others' ideas and expressing their own clearly and persuasively.

# *Conclusion*

As I write, my students have just returned from the New York State Capitol after debating educational bills on the floor of the legislature and meeting government officials with other young people across the state. This was part of a semester-long, project-based learning opportunity in their social studies class and the Youth and Government program of the Y. The organization's website describes Youth and Government as "a national program of the Y that involves thousands of teens nationwide in state-organized, model-government programs. Students have the opportunity to immerse themselves in experiential civic engagement and to practice democracy" (YMCA, n.d.).

At the start of the school year, students worked in teams to research and examine the current laws in education and think about what legislation was needed to make learning more successful. Throughout the semester, students learned about how the government works and researched ways to make education more accessible and successful for all learners. Students focused on scheduling conducive to the teenage brain, academic support for 21st century skills, technology initiatives, and on the forefront of all our concerns, school safety. Students spent weeks reading, writing proposals, creating surveys for the school community; and revising and preparing presentations for students, teachers, administrators, school board representatives, and congress. At the culmination of the project, five teams were selected as having pressing issues worthy of bringing to the state capitol. In the end, two students won special recognition for their ability to communicate their ideas and persuade government officials and their peers during the conference. This experience immersed students in literacy learning that put them in charge of their learning. Throughout the project, students embodied the ISTE Student Standards of Empowered Learner, Knowledge Constructor, Digital Citizen, Global Collaborator, Creative Communicator, and Computational Thinker (2016).

In order to prepare students for active participation in a global community, let alone a standardized test, students need to have world knowledge and strong communication skills. Thus, the world should be the driving curriculum in our schools. Assignments should be authentic, have real-world connections, and encourage students to create meaningful work similar to the Youth and Government program. Texts read in school need to go beyond fiction and nonfiction to include podcasts, popular culture, games, and films to help students think critically and create their own innovative artifacts. Technology has transformed the literacy landscape and is necessary in order to prepare our students for active engagement in a global democracy. It allows teachers to differentiate and support the diverse students in their classroom more readily with different apps and assistive technology. Students are able to collaborate online in their classrooms and around the globe in real time. Teachers and students have more versatility in learning inputs and outputs, involving audio, visual, digital, and written tools. Technology has enabled us all to access information more readily, while also facilitating critical and close reading of information—helping us to discern validity and bias, fact and fiction.

As Kasey Bell wrote, "technology is not a solution. It's an opportunity" (2018, p. 5). There are so many great tech tools to support students and learning, but thoughtful teaching and purpose need to be at the center of the conversation. We must address solid pedagogy that stands behind the technology, not simply fall prey to the siren song of the newest or fanciest tool. The current climate of education focuses on college and career readiness in the 21st century. To achieve this, students must read and write in school with real purpose, think critically, and formulate their own questions. Technology allows students to be informed, customize learning, and demonstrate learning in a variety of ways. Think about how you use technology and how those around you are using it. Then consider how you can use these same technology tools to learn, deepen student understanding, emphasize skills and strategies, articulate thinking, and look for clarity of ideas.

Writing is a vehicle for communication. Technology assists and amplifies the writer's voice, allowing students to author their own stories, tell their truth, and be heard. Today our students are bloggers, filmmakers, gamers, authors, innovators, and influencers. How amazing would it be to sharpen their strengths and abilities in our classrooms to create something that surpasses the standards and is ingenious?

So, what are you waiting for? Let's get started.

References

American Public Media. (2018). *Brains on* [Audio podcast]. Retrieved from brainson.org

Angel, R. (2011, September 29). Muse of nerds: Robots and creative writing. *WIRED*. Retrieved from wired.com/2011/09/muse-of-nerds-robots-and-creative-writing-2

Angelou, M. (1978). And still I rise [Spoken poetry]. Retrieved from youtube.com/watch?v=JqOqo5oLSZo&t=105s

Beals, M. P. (2007). *Warriors don't cry: A searing memoir of the battle to integrate Little Rock's Central High*. New York, NY: Scholastic.

Bell, K. (2018). *Shake up learning: Practical ideas to move from static to dynamic*. San Diego, CA: Dave Burgess Consulting.

Blei, M. & Zinger, T. (2017, October 8). MOTH storytelling workshop [Workshop]. Sponsored by National Council of Teachers of English, New York City, NY.

Bittman, M. (2011, March 15). Some animals are more equal than others. *The New York Times*. Retrieved from opinionator.blogs.nytimes.com/2011/03/15/some-animals-are-more-equal-than-others

Blei, M. (2018, July 24). Life and death on the Oregon Trail [Podcast]. *The Moth Radio Hour*. Retrieved from themoth.org/stories/life-and-death-on-the-oregon-trail

Bomer, K. (2016). *The journey is everything: Teaching essays that students want to write for people who want to read them*. Portsmouth, NH: Heinemann.

Burgess, D. (2012). *Teach like a pirate*. San Diego, CA: Dave Burgess Consulting.

Carroll, S. (Producer). (2015). What would Stephen Hawking do? [Podcast]. *Story Collider*. Retrieved from storycollider.org/stories/2016/1/1/sean-carroll-what-would-stephen-hawking-do

Cassinelli, C. (2018, August 29). Technology that sparks creativity, inspires interactive literacy projects. *School Library Journal*. Retrieved from slj.com/?detailStory=technology-that-sparks-creativity-inspires-interactive-literacy-projects

Coppola, S. (2017). *Renew! Being a better and more authentic writing teacher*. Portland, ME: Stenhouse Publishers.

Curtis, C.P. (1999). *Bud, not Buddy*. New York, NY: Delacorte Press.

Curts, E. (2017, April 8). Stop motion animation in Google Slides [Blog post]. *Control Alt Achieve*. Retrieved from controlaltachieve.com/2017/04/stop-motion-slides.html

Dewoskin, R. (2019). *Someday we will fly*. New York, NY: Viking.

Dickinson, E. (1998). Tell all the truth but tell it slant. In *The poems of Emily Dickinson: Reading edition*. Cambridge, MA: The Belknap Press of Harvard University Press. Retrieved from poetryfoundation.org/poems/56824/tell-all-the-truth-but-tell-it-slant-1263

Didriksen, E. (2015). *Pop sonnets: Shakespearean spins on your favorite songs*. New York, NY: Penguin.

Dillard, A. (1996). *Mornings like this: Found poems*. New York, NY: HarperCollins.

Docter, P. & Peterson, B. (Directors). (2009). *Up* [Motion picture]. USA: Pixar Animation Studios.

Doescher, I. (2013). *William Shakespeare's Star Wars*. Philadelphia, PA: Quirk Books.

Ea, P. (2015). "I am not black, you are not white" [Spoken word]. Retrieved from youtube.com/watch?v=q0qD2K2RWkc

Facing History and Ourselves. (2019). *About us*. Retrieved from facinghistory.org/about-us

Fisch, A. & Chenelle, S. (2014). *Using informational texts to teach* to kill a mockingbird. Lanham, MD: Rowman & Littlefield.

Fisher, D. & Frey, N. (2014). Student and teacher perspectives on a close reading protocol. *Literacy Research and Instruction, 53*(1), 25–49.

Fisher, J. (2013, November 1). When Tom McNichol saw swirling trash he launched his clean up boat. *Christian Science Monitor*. Retrieved from csmonitor.com/World/Making-a-difference/2013/1101/When-Tom-McNichol-saw-swirling-trash-he-launched-his-Clean-Up-Boat

Fitz, S. & Swartz, L. (2008). *The poetry experience*. Portland, ME: Stenhouse Publishers.

Flat Connections. (2019). *Flat connections* [Website]. Retrieved from flatconnections.com

Frank, A. (1967). *Anne Frank: The diary of a young girl*. Garden City, NY: Doubleday.

Frost, R. (1939). *The poetry of Robert Frost: The collected poems, complete and unabridged*. New York City, NY: Henry Holt and Company, Inc.

Gallagher, K. (2015). *In the best interest of students: Staying true to what works in the ELA classroom*. Portland, ME: Stenhouse Publishers.

Gallagher, K. & Kittle, P. (2018). *180 Days: Two teachers and the quest to engage and empower adolescents*. Portsmouth, NH: Heinemann.

Giff, P. R. (1997). *Lily's crossing*. New York, NY: Delacorte Press.

Gratz, A. (2017). *Refugee*. New York, NY: Scholastic.

Griggs, M. B. (2015, March 23). What goes in your toilet might be a literal goldmine. *Popular Science*. Retrieved from popsci.com/what-goes-your-toilet-might-be-literal-goldmine

Guardino, L. [LisaGuardino]. (2017, September 11). Revision gameboards... argument, informative & narrative writing #TsGiveTs http://goo.gl/Fr4XPr [Tweet]. Retrieved from twitter.com/LisaGuardino/status/907383240008142848

Gura, M. (2014). *Teaching literacy in the digital age: Inspiration for all levels and literacies*. Eugene, OR: International Society for Technology in Education.

Haiken, M. & Furman, L. R. (2018). *Personalized reading: Digital strategies and tools to support all learners*. Portland, OR: International Society for Technology in Education.

Hicks, T. (2013). *Crafting digital writing: composing texts across media and genres*. Portsmouth, NH: Heinemann.

Hicks, T. (2009). *The digital writing workshop*. Portsmouth, NH: Heinemann.

Highfill, L., Hilton, K., & Landis, S. (2016). *The HyperDoc handbook: Digital lesson design using Google Apps*. Irvine, CA: EdTechTeam.

Hochmann, J. & Wexler, N. (2017). *The writing revolution: A guide to advanced thinking through writing in all subjects and grades*. San Francisco, CA: Jossey-Bass.

Hoose, P. M. (2015). *The boys who challenged Hitler: Knud Pedersen and the Churchill Club*. New York, NY: Farrar, Straus, Giroux Books for Young Readers.

Houston, J. W. & Houston, J. (2012). *Farewell to Manzanar: A true story of Japanese American experience during and after the World War II internment*. New York, NY: Ember.

International Society for Technology in Education. (2017). *ISTE standards for educators*. Retrieved from iste.org/standards/for-educators

International Society for Technology in Education. (2016). *ISTE standards for students*. Retrieved from iste.org/standards/for-students

Iturbe, A. (2017). *The librarian of Auschwitz*. Solon, OH: Findaway World, LLC.

Jablonski, C. & Purvis, L. (2010). *Resistance: Book I*. New York, NY: First Second.

Kidd, S. M. (2010). *Long walk to water*. New York, NY: Clarion Books.

Koyczan, S. (2013, February). Shane Koyczan: To this day...for the bullied and beautiful [Video file]. Retrieved from ted.com/talks/shane_koyczan_to_this_day_for_the_bullied_and_beautiful?language=kk

Lamott, A. (1995). *Bird by bird: Some instructions on writing and life*. New York, NY: Anchor Books.

Lee, H. (1960). *To kill a mockingbird*. Philadelphia, PA: Lippincott.

Levine, K. (2002). *Hana's suitcase: A true story*. Toronto, Canada: Second Story Press.

Lowry, L. (1989). *Number the stars*. Boston, MA: Houghton Mifflin Co.

Mazzeo, T. (2016). *Irena's children: The extraordinary story of the woman who saved 2,500 children from the Warsaw ghetto*. New York, NY: Gallery Books.

McCarthy, C. & Blei, M. (2018, October 8). True stories told live: Exploring MOTH storytelling for teachers and students [Workshop]. New York City, NY.

McCloskey, S. (2018). *Doll-E 1.0*. Boston, MA: Little Brown and Co.

Merriam, E. (1990). New love. In Janeczko (Ed.) *The place my words are looking for: What poets say about and through their work*. New York, NY: Simon & Schuster Books for Young Readers.

Miranda, L. (2016). Hamilton: An American musical. In J. McCarter (Ed.), *Hamilton: The revolution*. New York, NY: Grand Central Publishing.

National Council for the Social Studies (NCSS). (2013). *The college, career, and civic life (C3) framework for social studies state standards: Guidance for enhancing the rigor of K-12 civics, economics, geography, and history*. Silver Spring, MD: NCSS.

National Governors Association Center for Best Practices & Council of Chief State School Officers. (2010). *Common core state standards for English language arts*. Retrieved from corestandards.org/ELA-Literacy

New Media Consortium & Consortium for School Networking. (2018). *Horizon report*. Austin, TX: The New Media Consortium.

New York State Board of Regents. (2017). *New York State Next Generation Standards for English Language Arts*. Albany, NY: New York State Education Department. Retrieved from nysed.gov/curriculum-instruction/new-york-state-next-generation-english-language-arts-learning-standards

New York Shakespeare Exchange. (2018). *The sonnet project*. Retrieved from nysx.org/programs-2/sonnet-project

The New York Times. (2017). A conversation on race. [Short film series]. Retrieved from nytimes.com/interactive/projects/your-stories/conversations-on-race

The New York Times. (2018, April 30). Op-docs: Information for filmmakers. *The New York Times*. Retrieved from nytimes.com/2018/04/30/opinion/about-op-docs.html

The New York Times. (2019). *Op-Docs video channel* [Webpage]. Retrieved from nytimes.com/video/op-docs

Norris, K. (1997). *The cloister walk*. New York, NY: Riverhead Books.

Oliver, M. (1992). The summer day. Retrieved from loc.gov/poetry/180/133.html

Orwell, G. (1990). *Animal farm*. New York, NY: Houghton Mifflin Books.

Ostriker, A. (1937). Dark matter and dark energy. Retrieved from poets.org/poetsorg/poem/dark-matter-and-dark-energy

Poetry Foundation. (n.d.). *Glossary of poetic terms*. Retrieved from poetryfoundation.org/learn/glossary-terms/limerick

Poetry Foundation. (2019). *Poetry Foundation*. [Website]. Retrieved from poetryfoundation.org

Poetry Slam, Inc. (n.d.). About PSi. Retrieved from poetryslam.com/about

Poetry Slam, Inc. (2019). *Poetry Slam, Inc*. [Website]. Retrieved from poetryslam.com

Pullinger, K. (2012). *Inanimate Alice*. Retrieved from inanimatealice.com

Randel, J. (2011). *Street smarts: Beyond the diploma*. Westport, CT: Rand Media Co.

Reynolds, L. (2012). A *call to creativity: Writing, reading, and inspiring students in an age of standardization*. New York, NY: Teachers College Press.

Robinson, K. (2006). Sir Ken Robinson: Do schools kill creativity? [Video file]. Retrieved from ted.com/talks/ken_robinson_says_schools_kill_creativity?language=en

Roche, P. (2014). 21 (CUPSI 2014) [Spoken poetry]. Retrieved from youtube.com/watch?v=6LnMhy8kDiQ

Romano, T. (2000). *Blending genres, altering styles*. Portsmouth, NH: Heinemann.

Schwartz, J. (2016, February 26). Decline of pollinators poses threat to world food supply, report says. *The New York Times*. Retrieved from nytimes.com/2016/02/27/science/decline-of-species-that-pollinate-poses-a-threat-to-global-food-supply-report-warns.html

Segura, A. & Gallagher, M. (Writers, Creators, and Co-Producers). (2018). *Lethal lit: A Tig Torres mystery* [Audio Podcast]. Retrieved from tigtorres.com

Sepetys, R. (2012). *Between shades of gray*. London, UK: Penguin Books.

Sepetys, R. (2016). *Salt of the sea*. New York, NY: Philomel Books.

Schwartz, K. (2016, July 28). How robots in English class can spark empathy and improve writing [Blog post]. Retrieved from kqed.org/mindshift/45834/how-robots-in-english-class-can-spark-empathy-and-improve-writing

Shakespeare, W. 1564–1616. (1998). *A midsummer night's dream*. New York, NY: Signet Classic.

Siegal, A. (2003). *Upon the head of the goat: A childhood in Hungary 1939–1944*. New York, NY: Square Fish Books.

Simmons, A. (2014, April 8). Why teaching poetry is so important. *The Atlantic*. Retrieved from theatlantic.com/education/archive/2014/04/why-teaching-poetry-is-so-important/360346

Spiegelman, A. (1986). *Maus: A survivor's tale*. New York, NY: Pantheon Books.

Spiegelman, A. (1991). *Maus II: A survivor's tale: And here my troubles began*. New York, NY: Pantheon Books.

Sterling, F. (2004). Study guide to the MTV film I'm still here: Real diaries of young people who lived during the Holocaust. *Facing History and Ourselves*. Retrieved from facinghistory.org/sites/default/files/publications/Salvaged Pages.pdf

Sundiata, S. (2006). Blink your eyes [Spoken poetry]. Retrieved from youtube.com/watch?v=RRonTMg3kbs

Tyson, N. (2019). *StarTalk radio show* [Podcast]. Retrieved from startalkradio.net

Van Allsburg, C. (1984). *The mysteries of Harris Burdick*. Boston, MA: Houghton Mifflin.

Vardell, S. & Wong, J. (2015). *The poetry of science: The poetry friday anthology for science for kids*. Princeton, NJ: Pomelo Books.

Worfolk, C. (2014). San Quentin's Giants [Documentary]. *The New York Times*. Retrieved from nytimes.com/video/opinion/100000003197035/san-quentins-giants.html

Watts, I. N. & Shoemaker, K. (1998). *Good-bye Marianne: A story of growing up in Nazi Germany*. Ontario, Canada: Tundra Books.

Wiesel, E. & Wiesel, M. (2008). *The night trilogy: Night, dawn, day*. New York, NY: Hill and Wang.

Wilson, K. (2019). *White rose*. Boston, MA: Versify.

YMCA. (n.d.). *Youth and government*. Retrieved from ymca.net/youthandgovernment

Zapruder, A. (2002). *Salvaged pages: Young writers' diaries of the Holocaust*. New Haven, CT: Yale University Press.

Index

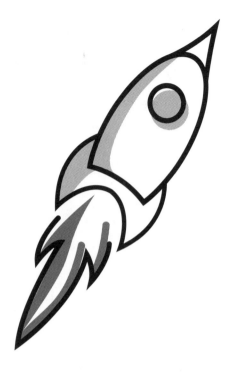

Your opinion matters: Tell us how we're doing!

Your feedback helps ISTE create the best possible resources for teaching and learning in the digital age. Share your thoughts with the community or tell us how we're doing!

You can:

✦ Write a review at amazon.com or barnesandnoble.com.

✦ Mention this book on social media and follow ISTE on Twitter @iste, Facebook @ISTEconnects or Instagram @isteconnects.

✦ Email us at books@iste.org with your questions or comments.